Biblical Studies from the Catholic Biblical Association of America

GENERAL EDITOR

FRANK J. MATERA

Previous Volumes in Biblical Studies from the CBA

THE THEOLOGY AND SPIRITUALITY OF THE PSALMS OF ASCENTS

BRADLEY C. GREGORY

Biblical Studies
from the Catholic Biblical
Association

No. 7

Paulist Press
New York / Mahwah, NJ

Cover image by Jerry Horbert / Shutterstock.com
Cover and book design by Lynn Else

Library of Congress Cataloging-in-Publication Data
Names: Gregory, Bradley C., author.
Title: The theology and spirituality of the Psalms of ascents / Bradley C. Gregory.
Description: New York / Mahwah, NJ : Paulist Press, [2022] | Series: Biblical studies from the Catholic Biblical Association of America ; no. 7 | Includes bibliographical references. | Summary: "This book provides an exploration of the theology and spirituality of the Psalms of Ascents (Psalms 120–134) with an emphasis on seeking the presence of God within a threatening and uncertain world" — Provided by publisher.
Identifiers: LCCN 2022005813 (print) | LCCN 2022005814 (ebook) | ISBN 9780809155538 (paperback) | ISBN 9781587689505 (ebook)
Subjects: LCSH: Bible. Psalms, CXX-CXXXIV—Criticism, interpretation, etc.
Classification: LCC BS1445.S6 G74 2022 (print) | LCC BS1445.S6 (ebook) | DDC 223/.206—dc23/eng/20220528
LC record available at https://lccn.loc.gov/2022005813
LC ebook record available at https://lccn.loc.gov/2022005814

ISBN 978-0-8091-5553-8 (paperback)
ISBN 978-1-58768-950-5 (e-book)

Published by Paulist Press
997 Macarthur Boulevard
Mahwah, New Jersey 07430
www.paulistpress.com

Printed and bound in the
United States of America

For Mendy

Contents

CONTENTS

About the Series

This series, Biblical Studies from the Catholic Biblical Association of America, seeks to bridge the gap between the technical exegetical work of the academic community and the educational and pastoral needs of the ecclesial community. Combining careful exegesis with a theological understanding of the text, the members of the Catholic Biblical Association of America have written these volumes in a style that is accessible to an educated, nonspecialized audience without compromising academic integrity.

These volumes deal with biblical texts and themes that are important and vital for the life and ministry of the Church. While some focus on specific biblical books or particular texts, others are concerned with important theological themes, still others with archaeological and geographical issues, and still others with questions of interpretation. Through this series, the members of the Catholic Biblical Association of America are eager to present the results of their research in a way that is relevant to an interested audience that goes beyond the confines of the academic community.

Preface

It will be helpful at the outset to clarify the aims of this book. According to chapter 3 of *Dei Verbum*, the Constitution on Divine Revelation from Vatican II, the project of scriptural interpretation should include both due attention to the meaning of a text within its original context and to how this meaning fits within the literary and theological context of the whole canon of Christian Scripture. In chapter 1 I explain more about this approach, but here I highlight that this is the interpretive framework within which I am self-consciously working. Those who, for various reasons, are committed to different interpretive frameworks will naturally disagree with some of my interpretive moves and conclusions, especially in chapter 5. In terms of the whole book, my working assumption for the Psalms of Ascents is that it is very likely that most, if not all, of these fifteen psalms should be dated to the Persian period and, regardless of the time of composition for each individual psalm, they were certainly brought together as a literary collection in the Persian period. The purpose of this book, then, is to explore how these psalms functioned in that historical and theological environment with an eye to their theological role in the whole of Christian Scripture. My discussions of each psalm are neither verse-by-verse commentaries nor a series of ahistorical "devotions" prompted by these psalms. They are, rather, an attempt to bring to the surface the theology that animates these psalms, both individually and as a literary collection, for those who first used them religiously during a pivotal time of sacred history. Likewise, by "spirituality" I do not mean something private or sentimental, but the lived reality of religious belief.[1] The addition of this term to the title of this book highlights the fact that the "theology" of the Psalms in their ancient context was never a merely academic affair but arose out of and shaped the actual religious life of their readers.

I would like to express my appreciation to the Catholic University of America for a sabbatical leave during which most of this book was written. I am also grateful to Enrique Aguilar, Gary Anderson, Joshua Benson, Bryan Gregory, Frank Matera, and an anonymous reviewer for reading part or all of the work and for their many helpful suggestions and critiques that considerably improved the book. I am also and especially grateful to Mendy, Benjamin, and Adelaide for their suggestions and encouragement.

Before moving on, a word about sources. There are a number of works that I have found particularly helpful for thinking about the Psalms of Ascents and their theology and to which I will sometimes refer. The full publication details for these may be found in the "Select Bibliography" at the end of the book.

---

1. For a fuller explanation of this definition of *spirituality*, see Michael J. Gorman, *Cruciformity: Paul's Narrative Spirituality of the Cross* (Grand Rapids: Eerdmans, 2001), 1–7.

CHAPTER 1

The Psalms of Ascents as Part of the Book of Psalms

WHAT ARE THE PSALMS?

Throughout the history of Christianity, the Book of Psalms has been one of the most read and loved books of the Old Testament. Virtually every kind of life experience and human emotion finds a counterpart in the Psalms, and so they have nourished, inspired, and guided the prayers and praise, as well as the theology and spirituality, of God's people for centuries. But what exactly are the Psalms? Where did they come from and what are Christians supposed to do with them? As intuitive as the answers to these questions might seem, the answers of readers have actually varied over the years.

One answer can be seen already in the New Testament and among many early Church fathers. Paralleling many Jewish interpreters in antiquity, early Christians often read the Psalms as prophetic literature that pointed forward to Christ, or at least were fulfilled in Christ. In Matthew 22:43–45, for example, Psalm 110 is portrayed as a prophecy of David about the coming Messiah. Some early Christians even saw prophetic significance in the *sequence* of certain psalms. Given that Psalm 22 is quoted by Jesus on the cross (Matt 27:46; Mark 15:34), some early Christian interpreters

like Origen and Didymus the Blind perceived a christological narrative sequence: Psalm 22 was a prophecy of the crucifixion; Psalm 23, with its reference to "the valley of the
shadow of death," was a prophecy of Christ's three days in
the grave; and Psalm 24 depicted the ascension of the "king
of glory" through the gates of heaven.[1]

A second answer, which has been present throughout
the history of the Church, is that the Psalms are liturgical
literature that is intended for worship, prayer, and spirituality. Of course, this approach can easily coexist alongside the
first answer since the Church views prayer, worship, and
the spiritual life as striving to conform the Christian into
the image of Christ. But the particular accent of this answer
is that the Psalms both reflect and facilitate a person's journey toward, and communion with, God. So, for example,
in his homily on Psalm 120, Augustine views the Psalms
of Ascents as describing the movement away from earthly,
temporal things to set one's affections solely on God. In
modern biblical scholarship this approach to the Psalms
tends to focus on the liturgical or spiritual use of the Psalms
in their original historical context. One of the most influential scholars of the twentieth century, Sigmund Mowinckel,
memorably described the Psalms as "the hymnbook of the
temple."[2] Many of the scholars pursuing this line of interpretation are mostly interested in reconstructing the features
of ancient Israel's liturgy, especially in comparison with the
religions of neighboring cultures, and they often leave open
the question of any abiding theological or spiritual import.
Liturgists, of course, have done much work on the ongoing
role of the Psalms in lectionaries and hymnals.

---

1. See Albert-Kees Geljon, "Didymus the Blind: Commentary on Psalm 24 (23 LXX): Introduction, Translation and Commentary," *Vigiliae Christianae* 65 (2011): 50–73.
2. Mowinckel, *The Psalms in Israel's Worship*, trans. D. R. Ap-Thomas, vol. 2 (Grand Rapids: Eerdmans, 2004 [orig. 1962]), 202–3.

A third answer highlights the nature of the Psalms *as a book that is to be read and studied,* that is, as a structured literary work, not just an anthology of prayers and hymns. In this vein, an essential part of the meaning of a particular psalm is found in its placement within the overall design of the Book of Psalms as well as in the relationship of the Psalms to the rest of Scripture. Concerning the latter, many modern scholars believe that the superscriptions of the Psalms were added later in order to connect them to events in Israel's sacred history. For example, the heading of Psalm 51 connects the penitence expressed there with David's sin with Bathsheba, thereby holding up as a model of repentance David's particular request for divine forgiveness after so great a sin. This, of course, assumes that the psalms of ancient Israel have *both* a particular historical context *and* an abiding theological and spiritual relevance for later readers who are invited to make these prayers and songs their own. Concerning the reading of individual psalms in their literary setting within the Book of Psalms, interpreters throughout history have noticed signs of intentional design. Jerome, like many modern scholars, viewed Psalm 1 as the introduction to the whole book (*Tractatus in librum Psalmos,* 3).[3] In fact, it is almost certainly not a coincidence that Psalm 1 correlates obedience to God's commands with a worshipful life and the whole Book of Psalms is divided into five "books" just like the Pentateuch: Psalms 1–41; Psalms 42–72; Psalms 73–89; Psalms 90–106; and Psalms 107–50. Notably, each of these five books ends with a colophon of praise, and the last five psalms of the whole book (Pss 146–50) punctuate

---

3. For a modern treatment that includes references to early and medieval interpreters, see C. L. Seow, "An Exquisitely Poetic Introduction to the Psalter," *JBL* 132 (2013): 275–93; and the longer treatment in Susan Gillingham, *A Journey of Two Psalms: The Reception of Psalms 1 and 2 in Jewish and Christian Tradition* (New York: Oxford University Press, 2013).

this movement with a finale of exuberant praise. These features as well as the fact that there is a noticeable overall shift in concentration from psalms of lament to psalms of praise as one moves through the book fully justify the Jewish title of the book, *Tehillim* ("Book of Praises").

What then are we to make of these different answers? What is the Book of Psalms and how should we read it? Let us start with an observation about a unique feature of the Psalms. While prophetic literature usually relates God's message to humans (e.g., "thus says the Lord") and narrative texts typically describe what God has done, the Psalms are somewhat different in that they are mostly presented as *human* words addressed directly *to God*. In this sense, the second answer above hits upon an important facet of the Psalms. These poems, hymns, and prayers were composed in real, concrete historical circumstances by people struggling, praising, challenging, and engaging with God. These psalms were then judged as fitting for other Jews (and later, Christians) to use as their own words to God, whether as part of temple worship or as part of personal devotion. And yet, precisely because they were viewed as having enduring theological and spiritual value, they were collected into a work whose arrangement is not haphazard or open-ended, but deliberate. As such, the third answer also hits upon an important aspect of the Psalms. The fact that these 150 psalms were collected and intentionally arranged into a book that became part of Scripture means that not only are they human words to God, but they are at the same time *God's word to humans*. In other words, these human words to God were recognized by Israel as *revelatory* of the divine-human relationship between the God of Israel and his people.

Yet, what about the prophetic dimension? While this approach has generally fallen out of favor with modern scholars, there is something valuable about this too. If we were to pose the straightforward question, "Are the Psalms about Christ?" there is a sense in which we would have to answer no. The authors of the Psalms were not envisioning Christ when they wrote and their goal was not to predict the future; rather, they were expressing their own faith (or their struggles with it) in their own circumstances, even if there are indeed places in the Psalms that resonate strongly with the life of Jesus and those places are pointed out by the New Testament authors. But in another, qualified sense, we can answer yes to this question, and in this the New Testament and the early Church fathers were onto something important. Just as a psalm should be interpreted within the context of the whole Book of Psalms, as Scripture it should also be interpreted in the context of the whole Christian canon.

A helpful analogy for what this might look like can be adapted from an illustration in a discussion of the proper interpretation of Scripture by the second-century bishop Irenaeus, in his work *Against Heresies*. Irenaeus compared Scripture to a mosaic in which each part is like a colorful tile (or jewel) that has its own shape, hue, and integrity that gives each tile value and importance all on its own. But when all the tiles of the mosaic are assembled in the proper way, they create a larger picture and that picture is of God as revealed in Jesus Christ.[4] Importantly, the tiles themselves are not changed from what they originally were, nor is their uniqueness lost when assembled. Rather, it is precisely the diversity and individuality of all the tiles that makes the larger picture possible when arranged properly. Likewise, while our commitment to respecting the original

---

4. Irenaeus likens those who wrongly interpret passages of Scripture to someone who disassembles the mosaic of a king and reassembles the pieces to produce a picture of a dog or a fox (*Against Heresies*, book 1, chaps. 8—9). A good edition of this work is Dominic J. Unger, trans., *St. Irenaeus of Lyons: Against the Heresies, Book I*, Ancient Christian Writers (Mahwah, NJ: Paulist Press, 1992). See 41–47 for this passage.

context and intentions of the Psalmists will not lead us to connect the Psalms to Christ in quite the same way as many earlier interpreters, we can still ask how these "tiles" contribute to the larger Scriptural portrait of Christ as the center and goal of all divine revelation. In this way, the original context and a christological reading are not so much in tension, as in fruitful dialogue and mutually enriching. The historical context does not exclude or invalidate the christological connections, nor should a christological reading overwhelm and displace the historical meaning. Instead, what is needed is an appreciation of the organic, dynamic relationship between these Old Testament texts and the New Testament proclamation of Jesus.[5] We will return to this idea more fully in chapter 5 in order to explore how to read the Psalms of Ascents as Christian Scripture.

WHAT ARE THE PSALMS OF ASCENTS?

One of the clearest signs that the Book of Psalms is not simply an anthology of disconnected psalms is the presence of distinct groupings within the book. Aside from several clusters of psalms attributed to David, there are also groups of psalms from temple guilds like the Asaphites (Pss 50, 73 – 83) as well as the Korahites and Ezrahites (Pss 42 – 49, 84 – 85, 87 – 89). Further, there are psalms that are clustered according to themes. For example, Psalms 93 – 106 put particular emphasis on the celebration of the kingship of

---

5. For some of the best examples of this approach, see the collection of studies in Gary A. Anderson, *Christian Doctrine and the Old Testament: Theology in the Service of Exegesis* (Grand Rapids: Baker Academic, 2017); and see especially his discussion of this dynamic regarding Mary and the Old Testament on 129–34.

Israel's God and his reign over the world, Israel, and salvation history.

However, perhaps the most intriguing cluster of psalms is situated almost at the center of the fifth and final "book" in Psalms (i.e., Pss 107—50) and is the only grouping in the whole Book of Psalms in which all the psalms of the group are placed together and appear one right after the other. There we find the peculiar collection of fifteen psalms, Psalms 120—34, which are united by a common superscription, "a song of ascents." This title has puzzled and fascinated readers since antiquity and there have been various proposals regarding what kind of upward journey is meant. One possibility is that the "ascents" refers to the literary features of these psalms as involving a kind of ascent. A striking feature of these psalms is that often an element at the end of one verse recurs at the beginning of the next verse, creating a kind of stair-stepping chain through the psalm. A good example of this is in Psalm 121. Verse 1 ends with "from whence shall come *my help?*" and verse 2 then begins "*My help* comes from the LORD." Similarly, verse 3 begins with the implied subject of God and ends with a depiction of God as "guardian." Verse 4 then picks up this same divine epithet at the beginning with "the guardian of Israel." Yet, as helpful and interesting as this observation is, scholars are agreed that this cannot be all that is meant by "ascents" because this kind of chain progression is found in plenty of other psalms as well. It is certainly a true feature of most of these psalms that contributes to the meaning and helps us appreciate their aesthetics, but there must be more to the title than just a kind of literary device.

The best, and by far the most common, view is that "ascents" refers to their use in the postexilic period as part of a physical journey toward Jerusalem. In the biblical world, Jerusalem was not just a location on a map, but in a deep theological sense the center and summit of the world. As the location of God's dwelling place on earth, it was the meeting place of the divine realm and the earthly realm and the orientation point around which all other things revolved. Therefore, regardless of one's geographic or topographic starting point, when moving toward Jerusalem one is always "going up" and when moving away from Jerusalem one is always "going down." Importantly, this is true regardless of whether one is moving north or south, east or west, or from a higher elevation to a lower elevation. What matters is whether one is physically moving toward or away from the place where God is encountered in a completely unique way. In other words, the idea of ascending is a *theological claim*, not an issue of cartography.

It could be that these psalms refer to a singular event in salvation history, namely the return from Babylonian exile in the late sixth century BCE. After the destruction of Jerusalem by the Babylonians in 586 BCE and decades in captivity, in 539 BCE the Persian leader Cyrus conquered Babylon and released the Jews to return to their homeland. This return is described as an ascent to Jerusalem in the Book of Ezra (see Ezra 1:3–5 and 7:9), and the interpersonal conflict in the Psalms of Ascents could plausibly reflect possible tensions between those returning from Babylon and those already in the land or between rival groups in Jerusalem. In addition, the end of the exile was certainly momentous enough to inspire its own collection of psalms and Psalm 126 makes explicit mention of the return from exile.

However, whether or not the return from exile may have been the specific catalyst for the composition of some of these psalms, a majority of scholars holds that the Psalms of Ascents were written for use during annual pilgrimages to Jerusalem. According to Deuteronomy 16, there are three yearly festivals that are not celebrated locally but require pilgrimage to Jerusalem: Passover, the Festival of Weeks (also known as Pentecost), and the Festival of Tabernacles. The first two are in the spring and Tabernacles occurs in the fall. Several features of the Psalms of Ascents suggest that the title refers to these annual pilgrimages and, more specifically, to the Festival of Tabernacles. First, with the exception of Psalm 132, the other fourteen psalms are all quite short, no more than nine verses with several that are just three or four verses. This fact along with the vivid imagery, the stair-stepping links mentioned above, and the repetition of phrases would have made these psalms relatively easy to memorize and then sing in community while traveling. The frequent alternation between the individual and the whole people also fits with the idea of individual pilgrims assembling as one people in Jerusalem. And the consistent focus in these psalms on the desire to encounter God in Zion makes good sense if that is the goal of the ascending journey. Second, the repeated use in these psalms of harvest imagery as part of the religious life accords well with the Festival of Tabernacles, which coincided with the fall harvest season. Finally, there is a very early Jewish tradition found in the Mishnah and the Tosefta that the fifteen Psalms of Ascents correspond to the singing that occurred during Tabernacles on the fifteen steps leading up to the temple.[6] While this could well have been a tradition that developed later, it provides some indirect corroboration that the Psalms of Ascents are best situated in the yearly pattern of pilgrimages to Jerusalem during the postexilic period. If we further consider the fact that the nature of the religious importance of Jerusalem's centrality was probably varied and contested during the Persian period, then the Psalms of Ascents may also have functioned as a theological ideal

---

6. The Mishnah and Tosefta are Jewish works from the second to third centuries CE that are edited compilations of Jewish legal and interpretive traditions.

of pilgrimage that served to *encourage* its audience to make these journeys.[7]

THE "SACRAMENTAL" THEOLOGY OF THE PSALMS OF ASCENTS

Here, though, we must be careful not to limit the setting and meaning of these psalms to merely a physical journey. For many modern people, religious belief and spirituality are a wholly internal matter that is largely independent of where we happen to be. Likewise, while the spiritual life may be affected by events in our lives, whether good or bad, modern people often do not see the spiritual life as inherently connected to any sort of steady rhythm of time. For this reason, it can be tempting to view these pilgrimage festivals as simply the setting of the psalms, but incidental to their theology and spirituality. But in ancient Israel, time and space could themselves be sacred. In Judaism there are patterns of time that are set apart as sacred and therefore different in essence from other times: the weekly Sabbath, the yearly festivals, the sabbatical years, the Jubilee, and so forth. These are not just times God's people are called to treat as sacred, but times that intrinsically are sacred. Times like the Sabbath and the seasonal festivals, which commemorated God's acts in history, were not just occasions that helped mark the passing of time but were periods or even realms imbued with greater cosmic and theological realities.

---

7.   See the careful study of the biblical and archaeological evidence regarding Jerusalem's religious centrality during the Persian period in Melody D. Knowles, *Centrality Practiced: Jerusalem in the Religious Practice of Yehud and the Diaspora in the Persian Period*, Archaeology and Biblical Studies 16 (Atlanta: Society of Biblical Literature, 2006), esp. her summary on 123.

Likewise, there is sacred space as well, with its apex at the temple in Jerusalem. The Temple Mount partakes of the sacredness of God's presence and radiates it out from there such that moving toward the temple is not simply exciting or a *prerequisite* for a spiritual experience, but is part of the unfolding spiritual experience. As Jon Levenson describes it,

> The Temple and its rites…can be conceived as the means for spiritual ascent from the lower to the higher realms, from a position distant from God to one in his very presence. The ascent of the Temple mount is a movement toward a higher degree of reality, one from the world as manifestation to the world as essence.[8]

Because worship in the temple represents the intersection of sacred space and sacred time, it is there the pilgrim discovers the world as it was intended by God: a personal communion between God and his people that is ordered around God's truth, goodness, and beauty.

On the other hand, as one journeys toward God in Jerusalem, there should be a corresponding spiritual journey that is interwoven with this physical, spatial reality. The pilgrimage itself, and not just its destination, is intended to be transformative. Because the pilgrims have set their eyes on Jerusalem, the whole journey is swept up into the transformative power of the God who is found there. Or to put it another way, because the pilgrims' hearts are set upon Jerusalem, the anticipation and movement involved in the journey make it an almost "sacramental" vehicle of God's goodness, grace, and blessing that draws the pilgrims along

---

8. Jon D. Levenson, *Sinai and Zion: An Entry into the Jewish Bible* (San Francisco: Harper & Row, 1985), 142.

as they seek, and are spiritually prepared to encounter, the presence of God. In this regard, it is notable that the exclamations "O Israel, hope in the Lord!" and "May the Lord bless you from Zion!" occur multiple times in the Psalms of Ascents, but nowhere else in the whole Old Testament. Yet, the fact that these are pilgrimage psalms implies that the worshipers will eventually return home, many of them away from Jerusalem. But there too the Psalms of Ascents are profound; for, there are hints in these psalms that the blessing experienced in Zion travels back with them to bless even the mundane aspects of life, awaiting further renewal on the next pilgrimage. This cycle of sacred time is representative of a spiritual life that ebbs and flows but is always rendered meaningful within the rhythms of Israel's worship.

From this vantage point the perspective of many of the Church fathers who saw the Psalms of Ascents as being primarily about the soul's journey to God is not off base, but complementary to the modern scholarly view of these psalms as pilgrimage psalms. In fact, their emphasis on the spiritual nature of the journey helps us to see another important dimension of the Psalms of Ascents. Their collection and incorporation into the Book of Psalms allows everyone, even those not on a physical pilgrimage, to participate in an analogous kind of spiritual ascent. Indeed, the inclusion of the Psalms of Ascents within Scripture creates a bridge from the specific context of those postexilic pilgrimages to a literary world that invites another pilgrimage by those who read them. And as we enter that literary world in the reading and study of the Psalms of Ascents, we are summoned to undertake a spiritual journey that is nourished by those ancient Jewish pilgrims who composed and sang these songs on their own journey toward God.

THE PSALMS OF ASCENTS

- ◆ A group of psalms (120–34) found all together and near the end of the Book of Psalms
- ◆ Were probably collected and purposefully arranged in the postexilic period for use in the pilgrimage festivals
- ◆ Reflect a "sacramental" theology in which physical pilgrimage and spiritual pilgrimage are interconnected
- ◆ Are animated by faith and hope that an encounter with God brings blessing, protection, and peace
- ◆ Should be interpreted in their own historical and literary context and then as part of the whole Christian canon

THE LITERARY JOURNEY IN THE PSALMS OF ASCENTS

For this reason, the theological and spiritual riches of the Psalms of Ascents cannot be fully grasped without attending to the literary progression of the psalms themselves. If their theology were to be treated only thematically, then their teaching might be understood, but the theological effect of traveling through these 101 verses would likely be missed. If one takes a global view of this collection, there are some strong indications of a thoughtful, deliberate arrangement. For example, the nineteenth-century scholar Ernst Hengstenberg and several others following him have pointed out that the middle psalm, Psalm 127, is attributed to Solomon, and on either side of it there are five anonymous psalms and two psalms attributed to David (Pss 122, 124, 131, and 133). Even more intriguing is that on either side of Psalm 127 the divine name occurs exactly twenty-four times and the shortened form of the divine name, *Yah*, occurs only twice, once each in the third psalm on each side (Pss 122:4 and 130:3).[9]

The most compelling analysis, and the one that will be followed here, is that of Erich Zenger.[10] He agrees that the unity and intentional literary arrangement of the Psalms of Ascents is indicated by the fact that there are so many literary connections and patterns between the psalms, including repeated echoes throughout the corpus of the Aaronic blessing in Numbers 6:24–26 (which, incidentally, has *fifteen* words in the Hebrew):

> The Lord bless you and keep you!
> The Lord let his face shine upon you, and be
>   gracious to you!
> The Lord look upon you kindly and give
>   you peace!

Zenger makes the intriguing suggestion that these fifteen psalms were selected and arranged from a group of Zion songs by those at the temple and for purchase as a short and portable souvenir "pilgrim's psalter" to be used by those traveling to and from Jerusalem on a yearly basis. If true, this theory helps explain why in different places the Psalms of Ascents seem designed both for private recitation and for public worship and why they view spirituality through the eyes of both the powerless and the privileged, as well as both the pilgrims and the priests.

Zenger argues that the Psalms of Ascents are arranged as three groups of five psalms: 120–24, 125–29, and 130–

---

9. Ernst W. Hengstenberg, *Commentary on the Psalms*, 3 vols., trans. P. Fairbairn and J. Thomson, vol. 3 (Edinburgh: T & T Clark, 1854), 409.

10. See Frank-Lothar Hossfeld and Erich Zenger, *Psalms 3: A Commentary on Psalms 101–150*, trans. Linda M. Maloney (Minneapolis: Fortress Press, 2011), 294–99.

34. The first and third groups begin with lament (Pss 120 and 130) and end with praise (Pss 124 and 134). The two psalms at the center of both groups, Psalms 122 and 132, reflect on God's choice of Jerusalem as the place both of God's temple and God's chosen king, David. The central group of five psalms, then, is Psalms 125 – 29. At the center is Psalm 127, which is a reminder that the ongoing vitality of Jerusalem and the temple is ultimately dependent on God's blessing. However, the outer psalms of this center group, Psalms 125 and 129, do not move from lament to praise like the first and third groups. Instead, in a brilliant stroke of artistry, they literarily mimic the overarching concern of the Psalms of Ascents in which God's people are threatened and surrounded by enemies and must rely on God for protection. Psalms 126 and 128 flank Psalm 127 with songs about God's blessing on those who rely on him. These are then "surrounded" by Psalms 125 and 129, which call out to God for protection against wicked enemies.

THE STRUCTURE OF THE PSALMS OF ASCENTS				
120	**121**	**122**	**123**	**124**
Lament		God's choice of Jerusalem		Praise
125	**126**	**127**	**128**	**129**
Protection from enemies	Blessing on those with faith	Need for God's blessing	Blessing on those with faith	Protection from enemies
130	**131**	**132**	**133**	**134**
Lament		God's choice of Jerusalem		Praise

Following Zenger's schema, we will take up each group of five psalms in the next three chapters, exploring the theology and spirituality of each psalm individually and as a cohesive group. Then in chapter 5 we will return to an overview of the theology and spirituality of this whole "pilgrim's psalter" to offer a rereading of them as Christian Scripture. There we will see that once these fifteen "tiles" are set within the "mosaic" of the whole Christian canon, a surprising paradox emerges: we will discover that our journey toward God was preceded by God's movement toward us. In our ascent we will encounter a God who has descended. As we lift our eyes to the heights, we will find a God of the depths (cf. Phil 2:7–8).

CONCLUSION

The Psalms are both human words to God and God's word to humans. As such they are intended to be read, studied, prayed, and sung. They are a rich source of theology and spirituality not just because they teach about God, but because they represent an inspired literary world that, when entered, can transform us as we encounter the God of Israel, supremely revealed in Jesus Christ. The Psalms of Ascents form a unique miniature psalter within the Book of Psalms that reflects postexilic Israel's confidence that in seeking God in Jerusalem the worshiper finds a blessing, protection, and peace that radiates out from Zion to infuse even the most quotidian aspects of everyday life. These psalms are a summons to a spirituality for priest and commoner, the powerful and the marginalized, those near and those far, and indeed anyone suspended between fear and hope on the journey toward God.

CHAPTER 2

The Search for Hope (Psalms 120 – 24)

It would be difficult to overstate the devastation wrought by the Babylonian exile. Before the Babylonians descended upon Jerusalem in the early sixth century BCE, God's people had spent several centuries in the promised land, under a royal dynasty stretching back to David, and with a temple where they encountered God in a way not possible anywhere else on earth. To be sure, there had been difficult times and almost constant threats, both external and internal, but they could point to these three things, land, king, and temple, as visible signs of God's beneficence and as distinguishing markers of their identity as a people. To be the people of God substantially meant to dwell in the land God had given them after bringing them out of Egypt, to be led by a dynasty to which God had made irrevocable promises to David (see 2 Sam 7), and to have privileged access to the very place where God had chosen to dwell on earth: the Jerusalem temple.

Then seemingly in a flash, the Babylonians swept away all of it. After toppling the Assyrian Empire in 612 BCE, the Babylonians stood virtually alone and unopposed across the Near Eastern world. Over the next few years, their imperial machinery established their own empire by steadily devouring one Assyrian vassal after another until they arrived at Jerusalem's gates in 597 BCE. As punishment for Jerusalem's initial refusal to accept the Babylonians as their new overlords, the current king from the line of David (Jehoiachin) and many of the prominent people in Jerusalem (including many priests and prophets) were hauled off as prisoners to Babylon. After a few more years the naïve advisors to the new puppet king Zedekiah provoked him to rebel against Babylon under the mistaken belief that because they were God's people and God dwelled in their temple, Jerusalem could never fall. That belief, which sounded so pious, was dismantled in 586 BCE when Nebuchadnezzar led his forces into Judea and laid siege to the city. With the people on the brink of starvation, the Babylonians eventually breached the walls, unleashed wholesale slaughter, burned the temple to the ground, and exiled scores of people into Babylonian captivity. With no land, no king, and no temple, the people were forced to ask some troubling questions: After such punishment for breaking the covenant, what could it even mean to be God's people anymore? And are we even still God's people anymore?

Into this vacuum of despair, pain, and fear stepped two key prophets who forged powerful visions of what a restoration of their lives would look like. They did this by going all the way back to Israel's theological foundations, drawing on images of creation and exodus. With evocative imagery Ezekiel said that God was not through with them, that he would move with incomprehensible power, grace, and creativity to bring new life to this desolated people and the "wasteland" of Judea (Ezek 36).[1] He drew on images of

---

1. These images represent prophetic flourish in order to portray the restoration as God's bringing life out of death. Historically speaking, Judea was not left completely barren and unpeopled by the Babylonians. See the classic study of Hans M. Barstad, *The Myth of the Empty Land: A Study in the History and Archaeology of Judah during the "Exilic" Period* (Oslo: Scandinavian University Press, 1996).

Adam in the Garden of Eden, of water flowing in the desert, of dead bones coming back to life, and of a miraculous, glorious temple to inspire the people who were struggling with hopelessness. A few decades later another prophet whose words are recorded in Isaiah 40 – 55 supplemented this hope with visions of a return that would be as dramatic as the exodus from Egypt. God would cast down Israel's oppressors and lead the Jews out of their captivity. He would guide them through the desert with miraculous provision of water and sustenance. He would bring them back home, redeem their suffering, and give them a new start. It all must have seemed auspiciously close when the Persian ruler Cyrus conquered Babylon in 539 BCE and permitted the people to return home to Jerusalem.

Yet, as the postexilic period unfolded, it looked quite different from these glorious prophetic visions. The overall perspective of biblical texts like Haggai, Zechariah, Ezra–Nehemiah, and Chronicles is that the period was disappointing. While there was initially excitement about a descendant of David named Zerubbabel, he vanished from the scene shortly thereafter. Although the temple was being rebuilt and sacrifice was being resumed, it did not seem to correspond to the picture Ezekiel had painted. And while they were back in the promised land, there were some difficult agricultural years and economic struggles. As one historian notes, "Most people lived at a subsistence level and would be considered in grinding poverty by modern standards."[2] The biblical texts also present a picture of social problems arising from struggles between those who

2. Lester L. Grabbe, *A History of the Jews and Judaism in the Second Temple Period*, vol. 1, *Yehud: A History of the Persian Province of Judah*, Library of Second Temple Studies 47 (New York: T&T Clark, 2004), 193.

returned from Babylon and the people already living there, as well as between rival groups in Jerusalem.[3]

On the other hand, despite the mostly bleak picture of the biblical sources, there were certainly some positive elements too. No period or set of circumstances is experienced or interpreted in the same way by everyone. What seems frightening or discouraging to some can seem exciting and hopeful to others. While many surely found the Persian period to be a time of hardship, for others the Persian period was no doubt a time of optimism, hope, and new possibilities. Although Jerusalem remained relatively small, there was also a vibrant religious creativity that produced texts and intellectual currents that would set the trajectory for Second Temple Judaism. Echoing Zechariah 4:6–10, Lester Grabbe nicely captures both the difficulties and the possibilities of the Persian period:

> The Persian period is important for the Jews because at that time the Jews were not important. Yehud was a small, backward province with a rural subsistence economy. Jerusalem, the only urban area, held still no more than a few thousand people at best. Judah did not occupy a strategic position from a geographical point of view and contributed only a small amount to imperial coffers. It could have disappeared from Persian history and no one would have noticed. The Persian period was important because it was a day

---

3. However, the archaeological record suggests that the return may have been more gradual, in which case the assimilation of the returnees may have involved less friction than suggested by the biblical texts. See Grabbe, *A History of the Jews and Judaism in the Second Temple Period*, 285–88, 356–58; Rainer Albertz, *Israel in Exile: The History and Literature of the Sixth Century B.C.E.*, trans. David Green (Atlanta: Society of Biblical Literature, 2003), 130–32.

of small things. Its accomplishments were not of might nor power but of the spirit.[4]

A significant part of this spiritual accomplishment is found in the Psalms of Ascents, which as a collection both reflects the wider biblical portrayal of the Persian period as one of hardship and strife while also giving voice to the spirit of hope and theological vibrancy that emerged during this period.

PSALM 120: LIVING IN EXILE

How does religious faith survive in a context of struggle and uncertainty? How does one find a way to God when discouragement and conflict have become common? It might have been tempting, as it often can be, to withdraw from what appears to be a frustratingly broken, fragmented world and to go it alone. One might try to forge a path to God through a spiritualization or individualization of belief that tries to hover above the real world and thereby insulate itself from vulnerability and therefore also from pain and discouragement. But that is not the way of the Psalms of Ascents. Here this miniature psalter begins its journey not in a theological idealism, but in the real world of conflict and spiritual anguish.

---

4. Grabbe, *A History of Jews and Judaism in the Second Temple Period*, 359–60.

o ☀ o

21

PSALM 120

¹ A song of ascents.

The LORD answered me
  when I called in my distress:
² LORD, deliver my soul from lying lips,
  from a treacherous tongue.
³ What will he inflict on you,
  O treacherous tongue,
  and what more besides?
⁴ A warrior's arrows
  sharpened with coals of brush wood!
⁵ Alas, I am a foreigner in Meshech,
  I live among the tents of Kedar!
⁶ Too long do I live
  among those who hate peace.
⁷ When I speak of peace,
  they are for war.

Psalm 120 begins promisingly enough with an affirmation that God did not remain silent in the face of the Psalmist's plea, but the nature of God's answer is left undescribed, which makes this psalm suitable for continual reuse in a variety of situations. A key problem for interpreting the psalm arises in that the rest of the psalm describes a conflict and asks God to deliver the Psalmist from it. How then does the situation in verses 2–7 relate to the distress mentioned in verse 1? One option is to see them as the same, in which case verses 2–7 would be a recollection of a situation in the past from which the Psalmist has already been delivered and is now expressing gratitude because of it. Yet, this would be odd for two reasons. First, the urgency, vividness, and length of verses 2–7 seem more appropriate to the Psalmist's current situation than to something that is no longer a concern. Second, in thanksgiving psalms, normally the celebration of God's intervention follows a description of the crisis rather than precedes it.

For this reason, most interpreters view verse 1 as describing God's pattern of behavior in the past, which then serves as the basis of confidence for the Psalmist's crying out again in his present crisis, which is described in verses 2–7. In this case Psalm 120 is a lament, but one in which there is an undercurrent of hope because God and the Psalmist have a history together. The Psalmist is in distress but not despair because he views his experience in light of the larger narrative arc of God's ongoing faithfulness. Their relationship does not shield him from trouble, but it does give him the confidence to pray in the midst of it. This will be a recurring motif throughout the Psalms of Ascents.

The rest of Psalm 120 shows that his trouble involves conflict with others. The Psalmist has been the victim of malicious slander and lying. Because one's family and social relationships were so important in the biblical world, sins of the tongue were often portrayed as a kind of violence. So, for example, Proverbs 25:18 warns, "A club, sword, or sharp arrow — the man who bears false witness against a neighbor." As such, the Psalmist is not just speaking about having his feelings hurt, but about the danger of having his life destroyed by enemies. It is curious that after speaking directly to God in verse 2, the Psalmist then turns to address the threatening tongue directly in verses 3–4. Yet, because the prayer has not broken off with verse 2, speaking to the tongue is not so much a switch of audience as an act of laying this interpersonal conflict before God. Rather than seeking his own vengeance, he prays that God would set things right. This is a wise move considering how poorly most people are able to weigh matters in which they are emotionally involved. In such cases, people usually overestimate the punishment that is due others and minimize their own role in the conflict.

Given how often in Scripture a malicious tongue is compared to weapons like arrows (see Ps 57:4), the punishment of the tongue described in verse 4 should be understood as a symmetrical "measure for measure" justice. The use of brush wood (from the broom shrub) was ideal for weapons because its hardness allows it to burn for a long time. Arrows fashioned with these coals could then ignite the target after the sharp point pierced it. This image adds to the symmetry since the wounds from lies and slander always sting at first but then also continue to burn and destroy long after the initial pain. The processing of his pain from interpersonal wounds in the presence of God means the Psalmist is trusting God for justice rather than indulging his own desire for vengeance. And so in verses 6–7 he will be able to claim honestly that he longs for peace.

The effect of this conflict on the Psalmist is profound. His exhaustion from the situation is clear from the use of "Alas!" in verse 5 and his claim in verse 6 that this has gone on for too long. He describes this experience of conflict as like being "a foreigner in Meshech" and living "among the tents of Kedar." According to other biblical references, Meshech was far to the north/northwest of Israel (near the Black Sea) and Kedar was to the south/southeast (in the Arabian desert). Both were legendary for their warlike belligerence (for Meshech, see Ezek 32:26; for Kedar, see Isa 21:13–17). Because these locations are so far away and in opposite directions, they are unlikely to be actual residences of the Psalmist; rather they are what Erich Zenger calls "theological topography."[5] If Jerusalem was the "center of the world" and associated with peace, order, and

---

5. Frank-Lothar Hossfeld and Erich Zenger, *Psalms 3: A Commentary on Psalms 101—150*, trans. Linda M. Maloney (Minneapolis: Fortress Press, 2011), 309.

harmony, then Meshech and Kedar are geographically its theological antonyms. Though part of God's people, the Psalmist feels about as far away from Zion as one can feel, as though he were at the borders of the inhabitable world, hemmed in on both sides from those who seek his destruction. It is possible to be in the promised land and to be experiencing exile, to be among God's people and to feel like a rejected outsider. But as the opening of the Psalms of Ascents, Psalm 120 also suggests that a sense of alienation can serve as a gateway to a journey toward God, no matter how far one feels from the desired destination.

Like the experience of this Psalmist, Israel's history was also a pattern of exiles and deliverances. Abraham, Isaac, and Jacob went through cycles of entering the land and being forced to leave, sometimes due to circumstances beyond their control and sometimes due to their own mistakes. The story of the nation of Israel began in Egyptian captivity, and then following the exodus they took up residence in the land. Eventually, due to their mounting sins, they were forced into exile in Babylon before being allowed to return under the Persians. But even though they were back in the land, it was easy to feel as though they were still in exile in some respects. Through it all, they were often hemmed in on all sides by those who threatened their destruction. And like the Psalmist, their only hope was the promise of God that he would hear the cry of his people (see, e.g., Exod 3:7–8). The Psalmist serves, then, as a type of Israel in that so much of faith requires holding together both a sense of one's own helplessness and a hope anchored in the faithfulness of God. This is the essential thing that allows one to lift one's gaze beyond the present distress.

PSALM 121: THE DESIRE FOR DIVINE HELP

In stark contrast to the sense of distress in Psalm 120, the tone changes in Psalm 121 to one of serene confidence. The reason for this is not that danger has passed, since this psalm also names various threats. Instead, the tone is different because Jerusalem, the earthly dwelling place of God, has now entered this Psalmist's vision.

PSALM 121

¹ A song of ascents.

I raise my eyes toward the mountains.
From whence shall come my help?
² My help comes from the LORD,
the maker of heaven and earth.
³ He will not allow your foot to slip;
or your guardian to sleep.
⁴ Behold, the guardian of Israel
never slumbers nor sleeps.
⁵ The LORD is your guardian;
The LORD is your shade
at your right hand.
⁶ By day the sun will not strike you,
nor the moon by night.
⁷ The LORD will guard you from all evil;
he will guard your soul.
⁸ The LORD will guard your coming and going
both now and forever.

The terrain of Israel is varied, but at the heart of the land it is very mountainous and nestled in these central mountains is Mount Zion, Jerusalem. Mountains themselves have an ambiguous quality. They can be places of danger or places of refuge; it all depends on what—or better, who—is in the mountains. Like life, the path through mountainous terrain often hides the view of what is just ahead until it is too late. A journey through the mountains can lead to ambush or to deliverance and so pilgrims would naturally feel both foreboding and hopefulness, perhaps careening from one to the other as their path unfolded before them. Yet both emotions would probably increase as they traveled deeper into the mountains and closer to Jerusalem. At some point, though, their destination, the holy city, would come into view and their perspective would be altered. The fact that the pilgrims don't just see Zion but "lift their eyes" evokes both desire and trust, directed at the God who will be encountered at the end of their journey. The helpless vulnerability all self-aware pilgrims naturally feel should prompt a contemplation of where true, reliable help may be found. No sooner has the question been asked than their vision itself supplies the answer: God is the only true source of help in a world of danger and unforeseen circumstances.

To this cry for help, verse 2 seems to provide the needed resolution. By using the liturgical formula "maker of heaven and earth," the Psalmist affirms that while God may be found in a unique way in Jerusalem, all the spaces outside of Jerusalem are also under his providential care. God's presence in Jerusalem does not preclude his involvement in the happenings outside of Jerusalem. And so, the one who is found in Jerusalem is also the one who created the surrounding mountains themselves, the roads through the mountains, the distant lands of the pilgrims' homes, indeed even the frightening territory of Meshech and Kedar, and so he can be trusted to care for these pilgrims as they undertake their journey from beginning to end.

One of the main problems in interpreting this psalm is the fact that verses 1–2 are in the first person ("I" and "my") but verses 3–8 are in the second person ("you" and "your"). While some interpreters have suggested that verses 3–8 represent an antiphonal response by a priest to the pilgrim who spoke in verses 1–2, others see the whole psalm as one of internal dialogue by the pilgrim who is reassuring himself of God's protection. On either approach, the confession of trust in God's help in verse 2 is followed by a contemplation of how this is so. Perhaps this need for reassurance suggests that pilgrims are often like the man in the Gospels who cried out, "I do believe, help my unbelief!" (Mark 9:24).

The reassurance of divine protection is artfully illustrated in verses 3–8 through a series of merisms. A merism is a common literary technique in the Bible in which two poles or extremes are paired as a way of signaling completeness. For example, in Revelation 21:6, Jesus says, "I am the Alpha and the Omega, the beginning and the end." Today we might say "from A to Z" or "from head to toe." In the second part of Psalm 121, God's protection is contemplated using interlocking merisms. The first takes up that which is below the pilgrims and that which is above the pilgrims. While God is said to be the "maker of heaven and earth" in verse 2, verses 3–6 take these up in reverse order: the earth below and then the heavens above. According to verse 3, God will not allow the pilgrim's foot to slip, which implies that God is not simply waiting in Jerusalem for the pilgrims to arrive but is actively involved in their journey toward him. In mountainous terrain a slip of footing can be disastrous or at least painful, but steps that do not slip almost always go unnoticed. How often must pilgrims have successfully arrived in Jerusalem and given thanks for protection from large threats, but never considered the grace that attended each of the thousands of steps it took to get there?

Then in verses 4–6, this protection is paired with a reassurance that God will protect the pilgrims from threats above, namely the sun and the moon. Many ancient people thought of the sun and moon not only as sources of light, but also as potential threats both physically and psychologically. The fact that God is able to provide protection ("shade") from these day and night, around the clock, is enabled by the fact that he never sleeps or even dozes off. This observation by the Psalmist is not simply a rhetorical flourish, because in other ancient Near Eastern religions gods routinely sleep and usually are aggravated if they are awoken. Israel's God, however, is like no other god. His continual protection also contrasts with the pilgrims themselves who may get tired, lose their concentration, and slip. Because God never gets tired and is ever vigilant, he is both capable and willing to protect the pilgrims from all threats (v. 7).

The Psalmist concludes with two final merisms related to time: "The LORD will guard your coming and going, both now and forever." As interpreters often point out, this lifts the gaze of the psalm beyond that of the single pilgrimage to encompass all of life. The LORD's protection is for the coming to Jerusalem and the going home, but also for all *other* comings and goings. It is both on this journey and for all those to come. This move at the end of the psalm takes the pilgrimage to Jerusalem and transforms it into a metaphor for all of life. Both the struggles and hardships as well as the hopes and divine care are emblematic of the whole arc of life as one that is a sojourning toward the presence of God.

In contemplating the nature of God's help on the pilgrimage, Psalm 121 pictures divine care as found below and above, day and night, on the road and in the soul, coming and going, now and forever. Just as threats are perceived on all sides, so the Psalmist feels enveloped by God's protection on all sides. The vertical and temporal imagery of Psalm 121 complements the horizontal and moral imagery of Psalm 120 to picture a world in which the Psalmists are reaching out for trust and hope in the midst of manifold threats. Reading Psalms 120–21 together suggests that however God's protection is to be understood, it cannot mean a complete exemption from distress. On a pilgrimage, instances of suffering and the experience of divine care cannot finally be mutually exclusive of one another. This tension, which animates the whole journey, can only find its resolution in the sacred space of Jerusalem, the place God has chosen, the city of peace.

PSALM 122: THE DIVINE CITY OF JOY AND PEACE

Psalm 122 stands at the center of the first group of the Psalms of Ascents and it is the first to be linked to a person, in this case David. In drawing the reader's mind back to David, the one who captured Jerusalem from the Jebusites and then brought the ark of the covenant there (2 Sam 5–6), the Psalmist takes the postexilic audience back to the beginning of Jerusalem's special role and evokes the figure of David as the first and prototypical pilgrim. From that point on, Jerusalem became the political, economic, social, and religious center of the Israelite people and a continual reminder of God's love for the greatest of Israel's kings. The postexilic audience would have felt itself a long way from that golden era, but they also would have seen in Jerusalem a latent promise of, and even a foretaste of, a more hopeful future.

PSALM 122

[1] A song of ascents. Of David.

I rejoiced when they said to me,
  "Let us go to the house of the LORD."
[2] And now our feet are standing
  within your gates, Jerusalem.
[3] Jerusalem, built as a city,
  walled round about.
[4] There the tribes go up,
  the tribes of the LORD,
As it was decreed for Israel,
  to give thanks to the name of the LORD.
[5] There are the thrones of justice,
  the thrones of the house of David.

[6] For the peace of Jerusalem pray:
  "May those who love you prosper!"
[7] May peace be within your ramparts,
  prosperity within your towers."
[8] For the sake of my brothers and friends I say,
  "Peace be with you."
[9] For the sake of the house of the LORD, our God,
  I pray for your good.

This psalm has drawn on the theology of preexilic "Songs of Zion," but has also transformed the tradition in light of postexilic realities. In earlier Zion songs such as Psalms 46, 48, 84, and 87, the greatness of Jerusalem was often portrayed in cosmic, mythic terms. Frequently these psalms took pleasure in pointing out the features and wonder of the city. In his book *Sinai and Zion*, Jon Levenson shows how this preexilic characterization of Jerusalem as the cosmic mountain had five features.[6] First, Zion was understood to be the center and reference point for the whole world. Second, it was the unique meeting place of heaven and earth. Third, it was a place of sacred time such that the present is infused with the realities of primordial time and eschatological time. Fourth, it was a place of order, not chaos, and so it was the world as it is supposed to be. And fifth, it transformed the people there to partake of its sacred nature. Because of these qualities, in the preexilic period Zion was often portrayed as invincible. As Psalm 46:6 succinctly puts it, "God is in its midst; it shall not be shaken."

These same features still can be seen in Psalm 122 but without the overtly cosmic, mythic elements. Jerusalem is still the center of Israel where all the tribes go up on pilgrimage for the festivals. It is still the site of justice, order, and peace. It is still the meeting place between heaven and earth in that God can be encountered and worshiped in the temple there. It is still the place where blessing can be received, and that inspires joy and awe. The direct address of Jerusalem in verse 2 as well as the mention of its gates, walls, ramparts, and towers in verses 2, 3, and 7 is reminiscent of the kind of affection in earlier Songs of Zion that delighted in the city's physical structures (see Ps 48:13–15). While Psalms 120 – 21 describe the pilgrim as enduring conflict and threats, Psalm 122:1 casts new light on this journey. Despite the costs such a trip would incur and the potential hardships faced, the thought of what awaits the pilgrim in Jerusalem stirs joy within him.

Yet, the understanding of Jerusalem in Psalm 122 also reflects a transformation brought about by the destruction of Jerusalem that led to the Babylonian exile. In place of the

---

6. See Jon D. Levenson, *Sinai and Zion: An Entry into the Jewish Bible* (San Francisco: Harper & Row, 1985), 115–37.

cosmic, mythic strength of Zion of the preexilic period, the focus has now shifted to the power of Jerusalem to unify and order communal life. Here, in contrast to the conflict of Psalm 120, the Psalmist picks up on the fact that a popular understanding of Jerusalem's name was "city of peace." Rather than cosmic forces, the chaos it now repels is that of conflict and injustice that arise out of the many possible disorderings of human life. The experience of the exile did not lead to an abandonment of Zion theology so much as a rethinking of the tradition to probe it deeper. As Jeremiah warned to those who believed Zion could never fall, it was always a mistake to believe mountains, walls, and fortifications were themselves sources of security (Jer 7:1–15). This mistake had led to a false presumption by some that covenant responsibilities to God and others could be safely ignored. Rather, what mattered was the God within those mountains, walls, and fortifications. God's special presence there was solely an expression of his commitment to live among a chosen people. The potential power of Zion must be understood in relational rather than geopolitical terms, as a vehicle for God's gracious condescension to dwell among his people.

However, even if the catastrophe of the exile did cause a transformation of Zion theology to deepen its covenantal significance, it still must be asked: During the postexilic period, how could such a vision have been credible? Zion had already fallen to the Babylonians and presently Jerusalem was subjugated to the Persian Empire. Some clearly felt that peace, prosperity, and justice were in short supply. In fact, Psalm 122 implicitly acknowledges this in verses 6–9 because it exhorts the pilgrims to pray for these things to come. This also gestures toward the answer. Jerusalem's power to forge unity and peace is not just something pilgrims come to receive, but something they are called to participate in and contribute to. As the place where all pilgrims come together to worship, it is already during the postexilic period a proleptic realization of this ideal. But the pilgrims come there not just to experience peace but to lend themselves to it.

The Jerusalem of Psalm 122 thereby functions as an icon of what the world should be and one day will be. But in the present, it can be only a partial inbreaking of that eschatological time of harmony. In the meantime, pilgrims enact their belief in Jerusalem's ultimate destiny by praying and seeking the peace of the city and all those who have assembled there. The realities of war, strife, and conflict may be real, but to seek God, to seek Jerusalem's peace, to seek justice is to bring a new, sacred reality into being. And so to enter Jerusalem with eyes of faith and to stand in its gates committed to its good is to enter the world as God intended it.

PSALM 123: COMPLETE DEPENDENCE ON GOD

Interpreters often note that Psalms 120–22 work well as a pilgrimage progression: beginning far away, then approaching Jerusalem, and then standing in Jerusalem's gates. There is less agreement regarding how (or even if) Psalms 123–24 relate to Psalms 120–22. If the pilgrims have arrived in Jerusalem by Psalm 122, what is left to sing about in the remaining psalms? The answer to this question has both a literary and a theological component. Literarily, as was discussed in the introduction, each group of five psalms places the climactic psalm of the group in the middle (Pss 122, 127, and 132) and uses the other psalms in the group to frame it. Theologically, Psalms 123–24 circle back and deepen the understanding of the spiritual issues at stake in the pilgrimage of Psalms 120 – 22 in a way that allows the overall progression of Psalms 120 – 24 to move from lament in Psalm 120 to praise in Psalm 124. However, while probing the spiritual issues of Psalms 120 – 22, Psalms 123 – 24 also raise a problem that will feature in Psalms 125 – 29: the tension between how things appear and the theological reality behind them.

PSALM 123

[1] A song of ascents.

To you I raise my eyes,
    to you enthroned in heaven.
[2] Yes, like the eyes of servants
    on the hand of their masters,
Like the eyes of a maid
    on the hand of her mistress,
So our eyes are on the Lord our God,
    till we are shown favor.
[3] Show us favor, Lord, show us favor,
    for we have our fill of contempt.
[4] Our souls are more than sated
    with mockery from the insolent,
    with contempt from the arrogant.

As in Psalm 121, the key action in this psalm is the raising of the eyes, but here this action is focused on God directly rather than on the mountains. The end of the psalm makes it clear that what the eyes perceive in front of the Psalmist is pain and conflict. The lifting then has the sense of a hope for deliverance from his present circumstances. It is an action that bespeaks a determination not to succumb to the tunnel vision that so often comes with suffering. The language of "have our fill" and "more than sated" in verses 3–4 echoes the exasperation of Psalm 120, where the Psalmist lamented that he was at the end of his rope in living among those who crave war and conflict rather than peace. Similarly, here there is the sense that the just intervention of God seems incomprehensibly delayed. The corrosive effect of this on the souls of the faithful calls out not just for explanation, but for divine relief. The feeling expressed in this psalm was surely familiar for some who were living during the Persian period. After generations of exile and oppression, it was difficult to see how divine kingship might be squared with the realities of the Persian period in which they remained subjected to Gentile overlords and some suffered at the hands of those within Israel who disregarded the demands of the covenant.

Yet, instead of becoming overwhelmed by what is in front of him, the Psalmist seeks a heavenly audience and perspective. What the Psalmist sees with the eyes of faith is that God is on the throne in heaven. The world is still under the sway of his rule even if the world around the Psalmist seems to have yielded the upper hand to the arrogant and insolent. It is one thing to believe that God is in control, that God is the Creator of the world and the master of its course through history; it is quite another to see this kingdom come on earth as it is in heaven and to find one's place in it. The ambiguity of what God's sovereignty means concretely for the Psalmist is deftly captured in the image of servants seeking their master in verse 2. In looking to the hand of their master, servants might be variously pleading, trusting, fearing, or inquiring. They might receive punishment, a command, a reward, or a gift. It all depends on the nature of the relationship between the master and the household servants. And when one is surrounded by enemies whose arrogance and insolence go unchecked, it can be tempting to conclude that the master, if he is truly in control, is hostile as well. But this Psalmist does not draw conclusions about the character of God based on the current character of the world. A hostile world does not imply a hostile God. Instead, the Psalmist trusts that what he will receive from God is favor, even if it seems delayed.

The question the reader is left with, though, is this: What does it mean to believe that God is in control and inclined toward favor when divine protection, vindication, and salvation seem so long in coming? This Psalmist gestures toward an answer in two ways. First, he lifts his eyes to God as the only one who can bring relief. The opening of the psalm places "to you" at the front of the verse to place emphasis on it with the connotation that the Psalmist turns his attention to God *and no one else*. And then in verse 3, for the first time in the Psalms of Ascents, the Psalmist speaks directly to God and requests the favor that is desperately needed. This shift to the second person in verses 3–4 is highly significant and is the second part of the answer: more important than receiving answers is the determination to stay engaged in the covenantal relationship. The fact that the Psalmist feels at the end of his rope does not lead him to abandon the relationship with God, but to continue to engage and have faith that God will respond. This is a common feature of biblical laments that is often overlooked. For example, in Psalm 89 the Psalmist confronts God with the reality that the promises to David in 2 Samuel 7 seem to have been shattered by the reality of the Babylonian exile. But instead of abandoning faith, the Psalmist pivots at the end of the psalm to plead for God to make it right because of who God is and the nature of his relationship with Israel. His voice of complaint is a sign that the relationship still matters and opens up a space in which he can continue to struggle with what he does not understand. Similarly, in

Psalm 123 the Psalmist's trusting petition for God to show favor is not just an expression of hope but can become a *source* for hope. By lifting his eyes to the one enthroned in heaven and engaging God directly, he begins to inculcate the kind of complete dependence on God that is essential for the furtherance of the covenantal relationship.

PSALM 124: GOD, OUR ONLY HOPE

The first group of five psalms in the Psalms of Ascents concludes with a psalm that revisits the familiar theme of danger, but now in a retrospective way that singles out God as the only reason the people survived what had looked to be certain destruction. As such, it completes the overall arc of the group from lament in Psalm 120 to praise in Psalm 124.

PSALM 124

[1] A song of ascents. Of David.

Had not the LORD been with us,
    let Israel say,
[2] Had not the LORD been with us,
    when people rose against us,
[3] Then they would have swallowed us alive,
    for their fury blazed against us.
[4] Then the waters would have engulfed us,
    the torrent overwhelmed us;
     [5] then seething water would have drowned us.
[6] Blessed is the LORD, who did not leave us
    to be torn by their teeth.
[7] We escaped with our lives like a bird
    from the fowler's snare;

  the snare was broken,
  and we escaped.
[8] Our help is in the name of the Lord,
  the maker of heaven and earth.

This psalm is intriguing because such thanksgiving for dramatic deliverance is more characteristic of individuals in the Psalms, but here the individual speaker in verse 1 summons the whole people of God to see their continued existence in these terms. Interpreters frequently note that the vivid imagery here is used by the prophets to describe the way the small and seemingly helpless nation of Israel was constantly threatened by the superpowers of the Near Eastern world. For example, Amos uses the imagery of uncontrollable fire and of predatory animals to describe military invasions and then applies it to the coming invasion of Israel by Assyria (Amos 1:7, 12, 14; 3:11–12). Isaiah uses the imagery of a torrent engulfing Jerusalem up to the neck to describe the invasion of the Assyrians in 701 BCE in which the whole country of Judah was overrun but Jerusalem was miraculously delivered (Isa 8:7–8). It is also intriguing that Assyrian records that have survived describe this same event as shutting up King Hezekiah "like a bird in a cage."[7] Further, Jeremiah describes the Babylonian leader Nebuchadnezzar as a mythical monster who devours and tears the flesh of Zion (Jer 51:34). And Ezekiel uses the imagery of ensnaring a bird for the Babylonian conquest of Jerusalem. In other words, the imagery that is piled up in Psalm 124 consists of well-known descriptions of the most threatening times in Israel's history: the fall of the Northern Kingdom to

---

7. This passage may be found in James B. Pritchard, *Ancient Near Eastern Texts Relating to the Old Testament*, 3rd ed. (Princeton, NJ: Princeton University Press, 1969), 287–88.

Assyria in 722 BCE, the invasion of the Southern Kingdom of Judah in 701 BCE, and the fall of the Southern Kingdom to Babylon in 586 BCE. On the national level, these images express catastrophic destruction but with overtones of chaos and seemingly unavoidable death. Plunged over and over into a world nearly undone and teetering on the precipice of the grave, Israel somehow miraculously survived each time.

It is almost irresistible to human nature to think about "what might have been," whether good or bad. For the Psalmist, the history of Israel serves as a reminder of the precariousness of life, for if any of those events had turned out just a little differently Israel could have disappeared from the scene. In 701 BCE, had Sennacherib not heard of trouble elsewhere in the empire (2 Kgs 19:7) or had his troops not been afflicted suddenly (2 Kgs 19:35), the siege of Jerusalem might have been completed and the people destroyed. In 586 BCE, had the Babylonians not resettled the exiled Jews together in Babylon allowing their culture to survive, the story of Israel might not have continued. But in contemplating these disasters, the emphasis does not fall on the disasters themselves, but on Israel's survival of them. Or to put it in salvation-historical terms, the Psalmist does not see in Israel's vulnerability to the nations a cause to question God's love; rather it is the survival of God's people through so many threats that demonstrates God's love. The approach of danger did not signal God's abandonment of the people but became an occasion of deliverance that naturally should lead to blessing the Lord (v. 6).

Because of its similarity to Psalm 121:2, many commentators consider verse 8 to be an editorial addition at the time this psalm was incorporated into the Psalms of Ascents. Even if so, it expresses well the theology of the psalm. For what is abundantly clear through the historical cycles of threat and suffering followed by deliverance and praise, is that Israel's very existence is a divine gift. Israel's repeated and mysterious emergence from the jaws of chaos and death points to the fact that the people's existence, past, present, and future, does not ultimately depend on their own efforts, but solely on the goodness of God. The maker of heaven and earth, the author of life, continues to conquer the forces of death in his covenant faithfulness to Israel.

CONCLUSION

A recurring theme in Psalms 120–24 is the experience of exile and hardship and the search for hope within the midst of it. In his discussions of the Psalms of Ascents, Augustine was fond of returning to a passage from an earlier pilgrimage psalm:

> Blessed the man who finds refuge in you,
>   in their hearts are pilgrim roads.
> As they pass through the Baca valley,
>   they find spring water to drink.
> The early rain covers it with blessings.
> They will go from strength to strength
>   and see the God of gods on Zion. (Ps 84:6–8)

Augustine noticed two important points from this passage. First, although the reference to the Baca valley is obscure, it seems to refer to a place characterized by dryness, hardship, and perhaps the danger that is found in an unknown wilderness. But when the pilgrim passes through this terrain, it is not necessarily because he has done something wrong or has made an error. Rather, it is the nature of pilgrimage itself that it will pass through a variety of conditions, some places of strength and some places of hardship. Passing through hardships is sometimes just constitutive of the journey. Second, the phrase "in their hearts are pilgrim roads" suggests not just that they are committed to the pilgrimage, but that the physical pilgrimage to Jerusalem mirrors that of human experience in general. Both the individual life and the historical, corporate life of Israel must pass along a variety of terrain and settings, and a period of trial or exile does not necessarily mean that God is either distant or hostile; rather it may be an unavoidable part of the journey. When the journey does pass over difficult terrain, sometimes all the pilgrims can do is lift their eyes to the only true source of hope and help, the God who faithfully shows favor to his chosen, who delivers his elect from mockery and contempt on all sides, and who brings life from certain death.

CHAPTER 3

The Search for the Center (Psalms 125 – 29)

The catastrophe of the exile and disappointments in the postexilic period when the prophets' visions failed to materialize as expected raised serious theological questions. With the collapse of the monarchy, the destruction of the temple, and the exile from the land, had God's covenant with Israel been nullified? If not, what would it look like now? Can meaning be found in disaster? When life does not turn out as expected, is this a sign that the tradition was wrong? Or that it must be rethought? Can righteousness and faith still be compelling when they do not seem to pay off? In the face of changing or even worsening circumstances, what kind of life is worth living?

One way of making sense of the Babylonian exile can be seen in Deuteronomy 4. There the exile is understood to be the just consequence for breaking the covenant and the remedy is for Israel to rededicate themselves to obedience. If they do, God will be quick to forgive and restore them. Another perspective can be seen in the Book of Isaiah. There the common image of fire as a metaphor for a destructive military attack, which we saw in Psalm 124 (also see Jer 4:4; 21:12; Ps 89:47), is transformed into an image of refining precious metals. From this angle, suffering can be redemptive because it can purify a remnant by removing the impurities of sin. For example, in Isaiah 48:10 God interprets the experience of the exile by saying, "See, I refined you, but not like silver; I tested you in the furnace of affliction."[1]

While this may have been true for the instance of the Babylonian exile, there is not always a clear "silver lining" to suffering. Indeed, even if these texts provide helpful perspectives on the exile in general, national terms, it becomes difficult to transfer these perspectives to the individual level. The very notion of a purified *remnant* implies that many did not survive the "fire" of the Babylonian invasion or the life in exile and still others had no chance to continue in the covenant. Further, this historical catastrophe was indiscriminate in falling upon Israel with the righteous suffering alongside the unrighteous. There were also plenty of people who were born and then died in exile who obviously could not have been morally responsible for the fall of Jerusalem and yet suffered the consequences anyway. Such incongruity between morality and the way life turned out continued to be noticed into the Persian period as well. For this reason some postexilic authors began to speak not just of Israel as a whole entity, but of Israel as comprising the just and faithful with those who were wicked and faithless now on the outside. Some of the latest portions of Isaiah, found in chapters 56–66, repeatedly make this distinction, but it is found in other postexilic texts too.

An interest in the theological problems raised by the exile can be seen especially in the Wisdom books. The Book of Job, which is usually dated to either the Babylonian or Persian period, wrestles with the problem of justice and suffering. In this book a righteous man named Job suffers

---

1. For other ways of making theological sense of the exile, see Rainer Albertz, *Israel in Exile: The History and Literature of the Sixth Century B.C.E.*, trans. David Green (Atlanta: Society of Biblical Literature, 2003), 4–44.

unbearable afflictions. While his friends Eliphaz, Bildad, and Zophar argue that in some way Job must bear responsibility since God is not unjust, Job refuses to deny what he knows is true: he is righteous but is suffering anyway. It is sometimes thought that the book's central question is "Why do the righteous suffer?" but this is actually not the main question; in fact, the character of Job never gets an explanation for why he has been suffering. Rather, the main question is that, given the fact that the righteous *do* suffer and there is no way to ensure one does not suffer through moral uprightness, is it still worth being righteous? The answer to that question is more complex, but the thrust of the Book of Job seems to be that yes, it is still good to "fear God and turn from evil," but not because it will guarantee a payoff. If it always did, humans would tend to reduce God to a transactional figure rather than an overwhelming presence before whom one can only stand in awe and deference.

A major upshot of a work like Job is that the world is far too complex and human insight far too limited to approach life with a kind of strategic calculus that labors under the illusion of control. The eyes of faith must often look beyond the way the world appears in order to grasp the way it really is, or better, the way God reveals it to be. Only once someone really understands that the true nature of the world is often different from the way it appears to a human with limited perspective can one begin to articulate what it means to live a good, meaningful life. This, of course, requires a belief that God is both good and faithful, even if one's experience of life in the present does not yet seem to bear that out. Living this way requires the union of faith and hope. The central group of psalms in the Psalms of Ascents aims at just this perspective.

45

PSALM 125:
AN UNSHAKEABLE FAITH

Psalm 125 is one of those unusual biblical texts for which placing it in its historical context actually makes its interpretation more complicated. This stems from the fact that at first blush the traditional understanding of Zion theology is readily apparent, but there are important differences from preexilic Zion songs that suggest a postexilic setting, and this renders its theological outlook more challenging.

PSALM 125

[1] A song of ascents.

Those trusting in the LORD are like Mount Zion,
    unshakable, forever enduring.
[2] As mountains surround Jerusalem,
    the LORD surrounds his people
    both now and forever.
[3] The scepter of the wicked will not prevail
    in the land allotted to the just,
Lest the just themselves
    turn their hands to evil.
[4] Do good, LORD, to the good,
    to those who are upright of heart.
[5] But those who turn aside to crooked ways
    may the LORD send down with the evildoers.
Peace upon Israel!

As was mentioned in the discussion of Psalm 122 in the last chapter, Zion songs like Psalms 46 and 48 typically portray Mount Zion as a cosmic mountain, that is, as the center of the world that is unassailable and able to hold the forces of chaos (i.e., the enemy nations) at bay. This view of Jerusalem seemed spectacularly confirmed when apparently unstoppable Assyrian forces laid siege to the city in 701 BCE but then were miraculously repelled. This quality of the holy city is simply assumed for the sake of comparison in verse 1, but to a postexilic audience this assumption had seemingly been disproved by the history that unfolded after 701. In 586 BCE the Babylonians had certainly shaken Mount Zion and razed it to the ground. In a lengthy and brutal siege their scepter had definitively prevailed and many of the people were swept into captivity in Babylon. Even after returning to the land under Cyrus the Persian in 539 BCE, there were times when it seemed that a scepter of unrighteousness hovered over the land. To make matters worse, Nehemiah 5 suggests that during the Persian period some suffered oppression, exploitation, and social injustice not just from the Persians but from wealthy and powerful Judeans as well. This distressing reality is reflected in Psalm 125 as well since it mentions "those who turn aside to crooked ways" alongside "the evildoers." It is generally agreed that the former refers to those among God's people who had ignored the demands of the covenant and sought to exploit their fellow Judeans. As verse 3 perceptively notes, the danger with such a situation is not just social in nature, but theological. If things are not set right, more and more of the just may be seduced to a morally bankrupt pragmatism. In other words, many among the Persian period audience had witnessed the very opposite of verses 1–3 come to pass in recent history: Zion had been toppled, the land overrun, and systems of injustice established. How, then, could such a people have possibly believed and sung Psalm 125?

One of the theological lessons of Israel's history is that it is a persistent temptation to grasp after divine gifts either as ends in themselves or as a subtle means to control God or the world. When God's people do that, the result is often disaster. For example, in 1 Samuel 4 the people of Israel are locked in battle with the Philistines. Thinking the ark of the covenant can be used like a talisman, the elders of Israel fetch it from Shiloh and bring it into battle only to lose the battle and, worse, to have the ark captured by the Philistines. Years later as the Babylonian threat loomed, many people in Jerusalem made the same mistake with respect to the temple, thinking that they could indulge in sin and injustice because Mount Zion provided an automatic source of protection. In what has come to be known as "the temple sermon," the prophet Jeremiah reminded them of the capture of the ark by the Philistines and warned them that believing that God's gifts could be leveraged against the responsibilities of the covenant was a grave miscalculation (Jer 7:1–15). As the Wisdom books show, the same tendency can be found in how people relate to the moral order. If they believe that good deeds will be rewarded, people can begin to treat God like a vending machine who is served or even placated merely to get what they want. If they believe they won't be rewarded, such people can see no compelling reason to obey God (see Wis 2:1–24). In each of these cases, whether it is the ark, Mount Zion, or the moral order, the fatal mistake is to treat God as the means and other things as the ends.

Psalm 125 demands from the reader what it also commends: unwavering trust in God despite the appearance of countervailing circumstances. The Psalmist has perceived that the theological significance of Mount Zion was about more than geographical coordinates, pillars, and walls; it was always more fundamentally about God's unshakeable commitment to live among a chosen people. To this end, the evocation of Zion's unshakeable endurance with all its cosmic and mythic overtones serves as an iconic window into the deeper theological reality. The plural "those trusting" in verse 1 has in view not so much "each individual who trusts" as it does the community whose defining characteristic is trust. From this angle, the shaking to the ground of the physical features that defined this relationship, namely the temple, the kingship, and the land, miraculously did not result in the disintegration of the chosen people; rather, God's faithfulness was on full display in the seemingly inexplicable survival of his people Israel, as highlighted in Psalm 124.

Yet, in such a context, faith is not easy. Psalm 125 readily concedes that in the present, injustice and wickedness can seem to prevail. But the Psalmist enacts his trust in God in three ways: first, he recognizes that ultimately the land belongs neither to the Persians nor even to the just; it is rather a gift from God he has "allotted" as a gift to his people (v. 3). Second, he boldly asks God to set things right, but leaves the timing in God's hands. Third, he ends with the salutation "Peace upon Israel!" Just as the characteristic of Zion's unshakeable firmness has now been transferred to the community of the faithful, so Jerusalem's essential quality of peace (see Ps 122:6–9) is wished upon the people who trust in God. This constitutes an expansion of the sacred space and sacred time of Zion in that wherever and whenever the community of faith is, they will find themselves surrounded by the God whose faithfulness to his people abides through all. The covenantal relationship between God and Israel truly is "unshakeable, forever enduring… both now and forever" (Ps 125:1–2).

PSALM 126: TEARS, THE SEED OF HOPE

Psalm 125 presents an image of the people surrounded by the Lord, metaphorically in the place of Zion and thus at the "center" of the world. In the next three psalms this dynamic is inverted in that these psalms give a picture of what life is like when one places the God of Israel at the center of it.

PSALM 126

¹ A song of ascents.

When the LORD restored the captives of Zion,
    we thought we were dreaming.
² Then our mouths were filled with laughter;
    our tongues sang for joy.
Then it was said among the nations,
    "The LORD had done great things for them."
³ The LORD has done great things for us;
    Oh, how happy we were!
⁴ Restore our captives, LORD,
    like the dry stream beds of the Negeb.

⁵ Those who sow in tears
    will reap with cries of joy.
⁶ Those who go forth weeping,
    carrying sacks of seed,
Will return with cries of joy,
    carrying their bundled sheaves.

Mark Twain is often credited with the saying, "History doesn't repeat itself, but it often rhymes." Whatever its actual source, this saying is an apt description of the history of Israel. From the journeys of the patriarchs, through the captivity in Egypt and the exodus, to the cycles of oppression and deliverance in the time of the judges, to the exiles of the Northern Kingdom to Assyria and of Judah to Babylon, the pattern of exile and trial followed by restoration and redemption serves as the ebb and flow of salvation history. Each instance has its distinctive characteristics, but the rhythm of exile and restoration creates a kind of historical rhyme in which each period can be understood in relation to previous and future points on this pattern of ebbs and flows. So, for example, the exodus from Egypt served as a type for the return from Babylonian exile as a "new exodus" in Isaiah 40 – 55, and then the original exodus and that "new exodus" in turn were used to picture the salvation Jesus brings in the Gospels (see, e.g., Mark 1:1–3).

When the postexilic period did not turn out as many expected, it was only natural that they would draw on these types and precedents from Israel's history to help interpret their own situation. In order to make sense of the fact that the people had been released from Babylon to return home in 539 BCE, and that a new temple had been built and sacrifices resumed, and yet the full glory of the promises of Ezekiel and the prophet in Isaiah 40 – 55 had not materialized, several works written during the postexilic period reveal a transformed understanding of exile and restoration that is then applied to their present circumstances. A good example is Ezra's prayer in Ezra 9. There he acknowledges the joy of returning from Babylon and rebuilding the temple, but he goes on to characterize the people's situation under Persia as, in some sense, a continuation of the exile. Scholars sometimes refer to this as the "theological exile" because even though the Jews were back in the land (and so, strictly speaking, no longer "exiled" in the traditional geographic sense of the word), the essential markers of restoration that the prophets described were still awaited. Restoration was partial but awaited a fuller realization.[2]

The idea that the people had experienced partial restoration but also were still in a kind of "theological exile" is at the heart of Psalm 126. In verses 1–3 the Psalmist reminisces about what it was like when they were restored from Babylon. After decades of mourning in exile, when some may have begun to think salvation would never come, suddenly all their fortunes began to change with Cyrus's victory over Babylon. Further, that, according to Ezra, he not only released them to return home, but also provided funds to rebuild the temple the Babylonians had destroyed must have seemed nearly too good to be true (Ezra 1:1–4). For so long Jerusalem and Mount Zion had seemed a distant memory, and now the exiles were arriving back in the land and watching with their own eyes as an altar was built, sacrifices were resumed, and the foundation of the temple began to be laid. Between the sound of construction, praise, and shouts of joy, the air was electric with the anticipation of the future the prophets had envisioned (Ezra 3:1–13). Even the nations took note (vv. 2–3). It was all like a dream.

Until it wasn't. The work on the temple soon sputtered and the reality of the Persian period struggles took hold. The postexilic reader of Psalm 126 knows this and so the recollection of verses 1–3 could be only bittersweet. It was such a promising start to restoration, but it now stood arrested as a continual reminder of what never completely came to be. It is important not to minimize the gap between verses 1–3 and what follows in verses 4–6. A postexilic worshiper could have completed the psalm begun in the first three verses with a more bitter ending,

---

2. See Michael Knibb, "The Exile in the Literature of the Intertestamental Period," *Heythrop Journal* 17 (1976): 253–79.

as in Psalm 89, or been tempted to despair at being disappointed once again.

Instead, the Psalmist addresses God directly with a hope inspired by God's continued faithfulness to restore Israel from captivity over and over again. Just as the Babylonian exile served as a type for the perception of a "theological exile" under Persia, so the redemption from exile, although only in part, served as a foundation for confidence that God would eventually bring complete restoration to his people. The Psalmist illustrates this hope by drawing from familiar death and life rhythms in nature. The first illustration appears in verse 4. The Negeb is the desert region on the southern end of Israel, which was parched during the dry season but in the rainy season its wadis would fill with life-giving water. The repeating cycle of dryness and water, which importantly is dependent on God and not subject to human control, is an image true to lived experience but also to the history of Israel. Periods of dryness eventually give way to the rush of water and new life.

The rhythm of death and new life is further developed in verses 5–6. The pair of sowing and reaping was a common illustration in Wisdom Literature because it nicely captures the complex relationship between the present and the future. On the one hand, certain seeds will produce certain crops; sunflower seeds produce sunflowers and not something else. And so "sowing" and "reaping" can be a way to affirm the justice of the world, that people tend to get what they deserve (see Prov 11:18; 22:8; Gal 6:7–8). On the other hand, sowing requires an element of sacrifice, risk, and faith. Farmers must make an investment in taking seed and sowing it in the ground because any number of things, such as a drought or pestilence, could ruin their harvest and leave them with nothing (see Eccl 11:6). Fruitfulness is not automatic but depends on divine provision (see Isa 30:23). Times of drought in the postexilic period made this abundantly clear, as when the prophet Haggai warned the people that because of their sin they had "sown much, but [had] brought in little" (Hag 1:6). Against this background, the sowing and reaping imagery of verses 5–6 is evocative. It is not simply that times of tears will eventually pass and be followed by times of joy and laughter, but that through divine provision, tears themselves lead to joy. The sacrifice and death involved in sowing, however incomprehensible in the present, can be redeemed to produce new life (John 12:24). And for the Psalmist it is precisely the restoration from Babylonian exile described in verses 1–3 that gives him the confidence to say not that these tears *might* lead to joy, but that they *will*. In the postexilic period Israel's pilgrimage at times passed through a terrain of tears. But instead of seeing in the unfulfilled promises of the prophets a reason to doubt God's faithfulness, the Psalmist finds in their tears the possibility of meaning and the seed of hope.

PSALM 127: GOD, THE SOURCE OF FLOURISHING

Psalm 127 stands at the center of the middle group of five psalms and therefore also at the center of the entire Psalms of Ascents. Here the theme shifts from living amidst hardship, even seeming failure, to a contemplation of the real source of success.

PSALM 127

¹ A song of ascents. Of Solomon.

Unless the LORD build the house,
    they labor in vain who build.
Unless the LORD guard the city,
    in vain does the guard keep watch.
² It is vain for you to rise early
    and put off your rest at night,
To eat bread earned by hard toil—
    all this God gives to his beloved in sleep.

³ Certainly sons are a gift from the LORD,
    the fruit of the womb, a reward.
⁴ Like arrows in the hand of a warrior
    are the sons born in one's youth.
⁵ Blessed is the man who has filled his quiver with them.
He will never be shamed
    for he will destroy his foes at the gate.

Apart from the heading "a song of ascents," it is difficult to see how this psalm, considered in insolation from its literary context, is related to the idea of pilgrimage. Most interpreters view it as essentially a Wisdom psalm about everyday life. In addition, the psalm seems to take up two distinct topics: house and city building in verses 1–2 and the growth of a family in verses 3–5. A closer look, though, shows that both halves of the psalm have a similar underlying theological perspective that connects them and also reveals the reason why this psalm has been placed at the very heart of the Psalms of Ascents. At root, this psalm is about the relationship between human effort and the divine gift of flourishing.

It is often pointed out that within the body of the psalm itself, the concern is only for the growth and security of a community (vv. 1–2) or a family (vv. 3–5) in a generic sense. The two parallel statements in verse 1 are not intended to dismiss the importance of human effort, but to emphasize the powerlessness of humans to guarantee their own success or to determine their own futures despite their best efforts. The verse presumes that builders will build and that watchmen will watch; these are indeed necessary but not sufficient for success. Humans are called to understand their own efforts as dependent on God's larger intentions. In verse 2, the Psalmist appeals to the daily reality of most ordinary ancient Jews: they get up early, work all day, and go to bed merely to provide for their most basic needs, only to repeat it all again the next day. And yet in the monotonous cycle of days, weeks, and years, the constant provision of the things necessary to rejuvenate the body, namely bread and sleep, is a divine gift. There is a strong undercurrent of thankfulness, not resignation, in these verses. The fact that human survival and flourishing are dependent on God is at the same time an indicator of human vulnerability but also of God's constant gratuitousness in even the smallest details of an ordinary life.

A similar point is made in verse 3. Unlike in many modern societies where children are sometimes seen as a burden, inconvenience, or at best an investment, in ancient Israel children were considered a blessing. This was not only because they could add to the family's labor force or because they could provide for aging parents in the future (though these were important), but also because they were considered a divine gift that allowed one's identity to be carried forward among God's people long after one had died. Children were a gift of life in more than one way. And yet, in the world of ancient Israel, infertility, infant mortality, tragedy, health hazards, and war often greatly hindered the ability for a family to grow. Figures like Abraham and Sarah, Ruth, and Hannah illustrate how securing a legacy of (many) children was not a sure thing. For a family, a tribe, or a people, extinction can always be just one generation away. During the Persian period when the community was small and vulnerable and Jerusalem was susceptible to attack, especially before the walls were rebuilt during the time of Nehemiah, the teaching of Psalm 127 would have been particularly poignant. Not just flourishing, but even survival, could not be presumed; they were utterly dependent on God for these.

For the postexilic audience of Psalm 127, the parallel between the precariousness of an individual family or city and that of the people of Israel was unmistakable. Such a small people, always wedged between much more powerful nations, constantly felt an imminent threat to their existence. Whether it was the Egyptian Pharaoh targeting all the Hebrew boys, or the Assyrian invasions, or the Babylonian conquest, or the Persian subjugation, Israel had learned well that they were often incapable in themselves of securing the protection of Jerusalem, its temple, or even their own survival as a people. In fact, the novella Esther, which is set in the Persian period, is about just this kind of existential threat to Israel's very existence. When Haman sets his mind to destroy the Jewish people, only the courage and wisdom of the providentially placed Esther and Mordecai circumvents the threat. In this story God's involvement in delivering the people can be difficult to detect at specific points in the story, but emerges more clearly, albeit subtly, when the whole narrative is viewed together. In this way, Israel's experience of closely averted disasters recapitulated the theme of the story of their forefather Isaac, who was bound to the altar with Abraham's blade perched above him, wondering if this was the end of God's promise. So also in their history, the people of Israel, the beloved "firstborn son of God" (see Exod 4:23; Hos 11:1) repeatedly found themselves in situations where it looked as though there was no hope for a future. Like Isaac they had come through not so much because of their own efforts, but because God was faithful to his promises and ensured their survival as a people.

This parallel between the life of an ordinary Jewish pilgrim and the continued existence of the whole people of Israel is what explains the incorporation of this psalm into the Psalms of Ascents. The superscription "of Solomon" probably means "about Solomon" rather than "by/from Solomon" and calls to mind the king who built Jerusalem's first temple. Its addition to this simple, idyllic psalm encourages the reader to view the psalm as having an additional meaning on the national level with the house evoking the temple ("the house of God"), the city evoking Jerusalem, and the family evoking the community of God's people. What is true of any single family and city is also true of the whole family of God and the city of God: they are called to cooperate in the work of creating and building, but with a humble awareness that the power to ensure their future will always elude them. This should not lead to hopelessness or apathy but to what is known in Ignatian spirituality as "indifference," namely a deep sense of freedom and openness to the future that is born of the recognition that everything is a divine gift and the future is wholly subject to divine wisdom rather than just human effort or calculation. From this vantage point, it is not only the powerful and influential who matter; even an ordinary family going about the routine business of their lives is endowed with a sacred significance if they are part of what God is building in each generation. To face the future with this kind of humble openness to God's designs epitomizes the kind of wise, pilgrim faith at the heart of the Psalms of Ascents.

PSALM 128: THE GOOD LIFE

As with the previous psalm, many interpreters view Psalm 128 as a Wisdom psalm because of its focus on traditional wisdom concepts like blessing, the fear of the Lord, and walking on the right path. But its orientation of these ideas around Zion situates these topics within the pilgrimage theology of the Psalms of Ascents. Theologically it also functions as a companion piece to Psalm 127. Both balance the idea that success in life is ultimately a divine gift with the importance of human action, but Psalm 127 puts the emphasis more on the former and Psalm 128 more on the latter.

PSALM 128

¹ A song of ascents.

Blessed are all who fear the LORD,
  and who walk in his ways.
² What your hands provide you will enjoy;
  you will be blessed and prosper:
³ Your wife will be like a fruitful vine
  within your home,
Your children like young olive plants
  around your table.
⁴ Just so will the man be blessed
  who fears the LORD.

⁵ May the Lᴏʀᴅ bless you from Zion;
   may you see Jerusalem's prosperity
   all the days of your life,
⁶ and live to see your children's children.
Peace upon Israel!

What does it mean to live a life that is "blessed," which is to say, a life that is happy, fulfilled, and good? The first claim the Psalmist makes is that blessing comes to those who "fear the Lord." This is an idiom found frequently among the ancient sages and some Psalmists that is a bigger idea than just the emotion "fear" applied to "the Lord," though there is an element of that involved. It is also more than simply reverence, though that is part of it as well. It is a disposition that flows out of the recognition of who God truly is and who humans are as his creatures. To have the "fear of the Lord" is to recognize that God is not just another character who occupies a role in the theater of our lives, but is the One who is all holy, all powerful, all good, and in whom all living creatures must find their point of orientation. To "fear the Lord" is to live with an awareness that all that humans are and do is *coram Deo*, before the presence of God, and therefore an absolute claim is made upon humans as those created in his image and for fellowship with him. This is why Scripture so frequently connects the fear of the Lord to obedience and "walking in his ways," as it does here in verse 1. In this way, walking the paths to Zion to obey the command to make pilgrimage to Jerusalem (see Ps 122:4) serves as a picture of how all of life is a process of walking toward God, in obedience to his ways, as the source and goal of life.

The emphasis on the fear of the Lord appears again in verse 4 in order to frame the picture of the fulfilled life that is painted in verses 2–3. Strikingly, the picture is a simple one of hard work that pays off and a family seated around the table. Given in terms familiar to the agricultural, patriarchal society of ancient Israel, it is a picture of contentment with the simple gifts of life, centered on the family as the fundamental unit of Jewish life. As Konrad Schaefer eloquently describes it, "the table [is] a sacrament of family unity and harmony" in which "the fruit of the father's labor is both around and on the table."[3] Such a picture is a reminder that life is embedded within one's family and one's community and so fearing the Lord and walking in his ways is not just individualistic piety, but *a way of being* in the world that produces peace and harmony.

However, all too often in the Persian period these simple pleasures were difficult to obtain for many ordinary Jewish people. Subjugated to their Persian overlords, some of what their hands produced necessarily contributed to the tribute paid to their masters. In lean times, ordinary people could get financially squeezed to the breaking point. The Book of Nehemiah reports how things came to a point of crisis and the people cried out that they had been forced to pawn their children, their fields, and their vineyards just to survive and still pay the royal taxes (Neh 5:1–5).[4] Against such a background, the promise in Psalm 128 serves as a poignant encouragement that somehow life can be made whole in the future. Psalm 128, like other Wisdom texts, does not offer such a vision as a kind of guaranteed, automatic exchange between obedience and God's reward. In fact, to turn these into transactional guarantees would be to reduce God to the human level and thereby to step outside of

---

3. Konrad Schaefer, *Psalms*, Berit Olam (Collegeville, MN: Liturgical Press, 2001), 308.

4. On the precarious position of subsistence workers in the Persian period, see Lester L. Grabbe, *A History of the Jews and Judaism in the Second Temple Period*, vol. 1, *Yehud: A History of the Persian Province of Judah*, Library of Second Temple Studies 47 (New York: T&T Clark, 2004), 172–73 and 205–8.

fearing the Lord. Instead, Psalm 128 offers an artistic appeal to the imagination that simultaneously accords a high level of dignity to an ordinary life well lived and holds out a promise that by walking in God's ways one can experience the blessings that God gives through the land and through the people, even if it is not apparent how this can be so.

The final two verses take up the concerns of verses 1–4 and broaden them. They are cast in the form of a priestly benediction (compare these verses with the Aaronic blessing in Num 6:24–26). Here the image of the children around the table is extended by a generation to one's children's children and the blessing is for "all the days of your life." Here the prosperity of the pilgrim is not in competition with the blessing of Jerusalem and the powerful who live there but is bound up with it. The harmony of the Jewish families and the peace of Israel go hand in hand. And further, it also reverses the image of the pilgrimage. At the festivals Jerusalem swells as pilgrims flow into it, but in Psalm 128 the blessings of Zion then flow back out into the ordinary lives of the pilgrims as they travel home and go about their daily lives, walking in the ways of God and learning to fear him.

PSALM 129: CRUSHED BUT NOT DESTROYED

From a literary point of view, it is ironic, but often true to life, that no sooner has the previous Psalmist wished peace upon Israel at the close of Psalm 128, that Psalm 129 opens with "viciously have they attacked me from my youth, let Israel say now." It seems to return the reader full circle to Psalm 125, when the scepter of the wicked held sway over the land. Nevertheless, the confidence that God's justice will win out at the end of the psalm is closely parallel to

Psalm 124, bringing the reader to a similar place at the end of both groups of five psalms.

PSALM 129

¹ A song of ascents.

Viciously have they attacked me from my youth,
    let Israel say now.
² Viciously have they attacked me from my youth,
    yet they have not prevailed against me.
³ Upon my back the plowers plowed,
    as they traced their long furrows.
⁴ But the just LORD cut me free
    from the ropes of the wicked.

⁵ May they recoil in disgrace,
    all who hate Zion.
⁶ May they be like grass on the rooftops
    withered in early growth,
⁷ Never to fill the reaper's hands,
    nor the arms of the binders of sheaves,
⁸ And with none passing by to call out:
    "The blessing of the LORD be upon you!
    We bless you in the name of the LORD!"

A common motif in the Old Testament, especially among the prophets, is the personification of the people of Israel as a single individual and sometimes even as the child of the Lord. For example, both Exodus and Hosea portray Israel as God's firstborn son whom he called out of captivity in Egypt (Exod 4:22; Hos 11:1). A particularly striking use of this motif is found in Isaiah 40–55, where Israel is portrayed as God's servant whom God called from within his mother's womb (Isa 42:1–9; 49:1–6). Yet, in this same text the servant sometimes appears as an individual within Israel who embodies Israel and whose suffering in exile leads to Israel's redemption (see 49:6; 50:4–11; 52:13 – 53:12). In Isaiah 40 – 55 there is a dynamic interplay between the personification of Israel as an individual and an individual who functions as a representative embodiment of all of Israel and who carries out a ministry on behalf of Israel.

In a similar way, Psalm 129 metaphorically casts Israel in the form of an individual person and salvation history in the form of this individual's life. Here in verses 1–2 this personified individual looks back to his "youth," which is a reference to the period of Egyptian captivity (for this idea see Hos 2:17; 11:1; Jer 2:2), and sees a long history of continual, brutal attacks. No sooner had one oppressor fallen that a new one rose to take his place. From Egyptian captivity to a series of enemies in the time of the Judges, to the Assyrian Empire, to the Babylonian Empire, and now to the Persian Empire, Israel had enjoyed very few periods of reprieve. Later readers could easily add Greece and Rome to the series of enemies. The imagery for this oppression, plowing this person's back, is a graphic portrayal of both pain and degradation. Isaiah 51:23 alludes to the practice of victorious kings walking on the backs of those they had conquered, and other prophets used agricultural illustrations of grinding, shredding, and digging to portray the brutality of war. For example, Amos compared the war crimes committed against Gilead to being ground down and broken apart by a threshing sledge (Amos 1:3) and Micah compares the destruction of Zion to being plowed like a field (Mic 3:12). According to the Psalmist here, this pattern of affliction has continued right up to the present.

This recurring pattern of foreign domination is distressing enough, but even more disturbing is how frequently such oppression came from within Israel itself. King Rehoboam, the son of Solomon, imposed harsh subjugation on his own people (1 Kgs 12:13–15). Amos decried the powerful people within Israel who exploit the poor and "trample the heads of the destitute into the dust of the earth" (Amos 2:7). Examples could be multiplied. Commentators both ancient and modern have often pointed out that, as in Psalm 120, it is difficult to decide whether the attackers here in Psalm 129 are solely those outside of Israel or also include those within Israel, but the fact that both are plausible is itself sobering. In his commentary on this psalm, Augustine sadly observed that it remains the same in the Church and will remain so until the end when the wheat and the tares are finally separated (see Matt 13:24–30). Wounds on the people of God inflicted from within the people of God are often more damaging and painful than those from any external persecutor.

Yet, as graphic and dispiriting as verses 1–3 are, there is a flip side to this history: all of these oppressors ultimately, eventually did not prevail. It is not that Israel had conquered them, but that they had survived them. God's presence and love for Israel is discerned in their mysterious resilience while other, more powerful kingdoms eventually fade from history. Empires rise and fall, but the much smaller Israel endures. And so the Psalmist recognizes in verse 4 that each time it was God who set Israel free. The picture is of Israel under a yoke of bondage and the oppressors using cords attached to the yoke to subdue and control them (see Isa 9:4; Ezek 34:27). Breaking these cords represents an act of deliverance.

As is typical in God's economy, deliverance is accompanied by the enactment of justice, which in verses 5–8 is full of irony. Those who plowed are now just withered produce that is useless to the reapers. They are like grass that appears to occupy a lofty place since it is on the rooftops but, in reality, is doomed from the start precisely because of being set on high. By trying to take root in faulty, inhospitable soil, they set themselves up to be powerless before the heat of the sun and will soon come to nothing. Importantly, the nature of the arrival of this justice in verses 5–6 is not completely clear. The Hebrew may equally be read as a wish/petition, that is, "may they recoil in disgrace," or as a statement of fact, that is, "they will recoil in disgrace," and commentators disagree about which sense is most likely. Either way, the psalm can be prayed by anyone longing for God's justice, regardless of how much or little confidence their hope contains.

The NABRE translates verses 5–8 as a wish or petition, which raises the question of whether it can ever be appropriate to pray for harm on one's enemies. This is a thorny problem of interpretation, but it should be highlighted that texts like Psalm 129 are at least realistic about human experience. Anyone who has suffered greatly at the hands of others understands the importance of naming injustices for what they are and calling those who perpetrate them to account. These psalms do not counsel a kind of "forgetting and moving on" that glosses over and buries the reality of violence, but rather bring the outrage to the surface. Second, and equally important, is that while these emotions are expressed, they are nevertheless processed in the context of prayer rather than in seeking personal vengeance. It is highly significant that the Psalmist entrusts the matter to God's hands and defers to God's timing. Third, the symmetry created between the agricultural imagery in verses 1–4 and in verses 5–8 shows that the Psalmist primarily seeks the establishment of equitable justice rather than merely the suffering of the oppressors. This is important because humans sometimes overestimate the punishment due to others and can easily set in motion a cycle of vengeance that just continues to escalate. History has shown that it is all too easy for the oppressed to become oppressors as soon as the tables are turned. In the face of repeated injustice the Psalmist does not conclude that God is absent, uncaring, or malevolent, nor does he conclude that he must take matters into his own hands. Instead, he cries out for things to be set right and thereby displays confident faith that God really is at work to bring both salvation and justice, even though at the present time violence and evil remain in the world.[5]

CONCLUSION

Religious belief often approaches a crossroad when life turns out differently from one's expectations and seems to run counter to one's theology. For some the Babylonian exile and disappointments in the Persian period represented back-to-back challenges to Israel's self-understanding as the people of God. The confusion that flows from repeated disaster and disappointment presses the question: How can people have an unshakeable faith when the scepter of unrighteousness seems to prevail (Ps 125) and the backs of the just are being plowed by the wicked (Ps 129)?

A notable feature of the Psalms of Ascents is that they do not try to rationalize or explain away the presence of injustice or suffering. There is a dual danger in trying to insist that the world must be fair. One is that when it inevitably is not, belief in God, or at least God's goodness, is prone

---

5. For further discussion of this difficult theological topic, I especially recommend Gary A. Anderson, "King David and the Psalms of Imprecation," *Pro Ecclesia* 15 (2006): 267–80. Also see the sensitive reflection on Psalm 137 by Pope Benedict XVI in his general address of November 30, 2005 (available online at https://www.vatican.va/content/benedict-xvi/en/audiences/2005/documents/hf_ben-xvi_aud_20051130.html).

to be abandoned. The second is that it risks reducing God to a transactional character with whom humans engage in an exchange of service and reward. This can easily become a mechanism for trying to control God by demanding that he behave in certain ways in response to human actions.

Viewed against the Persian period background, Psalms 125–29 do not try to provide an explanation for the theological problems of the experiences of exile and injustice; rather, they model a way of living faithfully in the midst of these problems. Yet, the challenge of living faithfully is accentuated by the fact it often must be undertaken even when present circumstances cannot be resolved or even completely understood. As pilgrims lift their eyes to the mountains of Jerusalem to focus on the divine source of their help (Ps 121:1), so Psalms 125–29 seek to refocus or recalibrate one's theological vision to see the more profound reality behind the present appearances.

These five psalms recalibrate one's theological vision in several ways. First, they interpret the Psalmist's present crisis in light of the long arc of Israel's history and the patterns of exile and restoration that structure it. Eventually, justice will be established and oppressors and the wicked will recoil in disgrace and wither into insignificance. Those who trust in the Lord will flourish and prosper, enjoying the fruits of lives well lived. Yet crucially, this flourishing is not just because oppression and wickedness have ceased or have been removed, but because the suffering of those times will be redeemed. Sowing in tears carries within itself the power of hope that joyful reaping is surely coming. The dreams of former times can nourish the dreams of the future.

Second, the fact that Israel's history "rhymes" more than it repeats means that Israel is not simply caught in a repetitive cycle of exiles and restorations. It is more like a spiral that is heading somewhere. Each point in history resonates with similar past and future points but is itself still distinct. This allows a certain theological malleability to the traditions of the past as they are drawn upon to speak to new points on this historical spiral. What was formerly theologically believed about Zion can now be reapplied to the community of faith. The peace and blessing anchored in the sacred space of Zion is now understood to flow back out to the people of Israel, wherever they live and however ordinary their lives appear to be. At times, these psalms contain an eschatological, almost prophetic, outlook that by faith holds that the life of Israel as the community of God's chosen people will eventually be resolved into peace and blessing when the spiral reaches its consummation.

Third, central to both of these convictions is the divine-human dynamic that is expressed in the central psalm, Psalm 127. In the present time, even if justice seems not to reign, those with faith are called nevertheless to work, to build, to guard, to produce, but also to relinquish to God any aspirations of control over the results. Faith and hope are possible only when God is acknowledged as incomparably supreme and therefore at the center of life. This requires an openness to divine freedom that accepts the uncertainty of life and affirms that all is a divine gift. As Ambrose comments on the similar theme in Psalm 73,

> No one can truly proclaim that God is good but one who knows that goodness is not from his own successes and profits but out of the depth of the heavenly mysteries and the height of God's plan. For it is to be weighed not by the appearance of things present but by the advantage of things to

come. Consequently, to the just person God is always good.[6]

This is ultimately what it means to fear the Lord and walk in his ways. It is the only way that faith and hope can be unshakably united.

---

6.   Quoted in Quentin F Wesselschmidt, *Psalms 51—150*, Ancient Christian Commentary on Scripture (Downers Grove, IL: InterVarsity Press, 2007), 101.

CHAPTER 4

The Search for Wholeness (Psalms 130 – 34)

Compared to the first ten psalms in the Psalms of Ascents, Psalms 130 – 34 are more concerned with the interior character qualities of the religious life of pilgrimage. Building on the emphasis in Psalms 125 – 29 on placing God at the center of life, these last five psalms unfold the paradoxical idea that the lowering of oneself is an indispensable part of religious ascent. This biblical truth stands in marked contrast to the assumption of many modern people that a focus on the self (or even self-absorption) is essential to finding personal wholeness.

Deep within Israel's understanding of their own identity was an awareness that based solely on their own nature and abilities they could neither expect nor justify their own continued existence or God's faithful dealings with them. The stories of the patriarchs and matriarchs in Genesis reminded them of how precarious their existence could be. Were it not for God's interventions at crucial moments in the story, the promises to Abraham surely would have come to naught. Whether it was from severe famine or Pharaoh's interest in Sarah or the near sacrifice of Isaac, the ongoing existence of Abraham's family was dependent on God's gracious deliverance amidst what seemed like hopeless circumstances. This continued in Israel's later history as the

71

people were repeatedly on the brink of possible disaster, sometimes because of their own sin and sometimes merely because of the unfortunate turns of history. Sometimes they averted disaster and sometimes they were plunged into it, but in each case, it was never the end of Israel's story because God would not let it be. He remained faithful to his promises to Abraham, Isaac, and Jacob even when his people proved faithless again.

The quintessential example of this was the golden calf incident in Exodus 32–34. The people had been rescued from the oppression of Egypt because of God's faithfulness to the promises to the patriarchs (Exod 3:5-10). Once they were free, God directed them to Mount Sinai to enter into a covenant with them. However, despite just agreeing to enter into a covenantal relationship with God, Israel made a golden calf and worshiped it almost as soon as Moses went back up Mount Sinai to get design plans for the tabernacle. While God was making plans to dwell among his people, these same people were breaking the covenant they had just agreed to and in the most egregious way imaginable. Yet when Moses once again reminded God of his promises to Abraham, Isaac, and Jacob, he relented from his intention to destroy Israel and their story continued on. This incident served as a constant reminder throughout Israel's history that no matter how faithless they were, God would never prove faithless. Their survival from all threats, both external and internal, has always been due primarily to God's faithfulness.

A central theme of Deuteronomy 1–11 is the primacy of grace: Israel was chosen not because they had anything in themselves to offer, but because God chose Abraham, Isaac, and Jacob and set his love on them and their descendants. Like the poor and lowly, Israel was small, often vulnerable, and dependent on God; in each generation, then, it owed its very existence to God. It was because of this grace that Israel was called to obey the covenant and walk in the ways of the Lord. Israel's covenantal relationship with God was dramatically asymmetrical; it was between a great, holy, and gracious God and a small and unworthy people. Therefore, since the beginning, humility and obedience have always been understood as two sides of the same coin.

Conversely, sin and rebellion often go hand in hand with an arrogant forgetfulness of who one is before the presence of God. In fact, throughout the Old Testament there is a series of mythic stories about powerful humans who arrogate to themselves the power to act independently of, or even in opposition to, God.[1] In Genesis 11 the people of Babel decided to make a name for themselves by building a city and tower to the heavens. In Exodus 5 Pharaoh arrogated to himself complete rights over Israel and scoffed at God's claim on his people. In Isaiah 14 the king of Babylon aspired to ascend to heaven and establish his throne above the stars of God. In Ezekiel 28 the prince of Tyre believed himself to be divine and so undertook all kinds of lawlessness. Later the Greek tyrant Antiochus IV Epiphanes would be remembered in a similar way (Dan 7; 2 Macc 9). In each of these cases, the attempt to usurp God's place as the one in control of the world resulted in God's casting them down in judgment. This is why Israel's sages repeatedly warned that "pride goes before disaster, and a haughty spirit before a fall" (Prov 16:18; also see Prov 11:2; 29:23; Sir 10:12–18).

In fact, the same pattern of pride and power could be seen in Israel's own history. Prophets like Hosea and Jeremiah concluded that it was arrogance that led the

---

1. For the theological importance of these stories for the Old Testament's understanding of humanity, see Donald Gowan, *When Man Becomes God: Humanism and Hybris in the Old Testament*, Princeton Theological Monograph Series (Eugene, OR: Pickwick, 1975).

Northern Kingdom and then the Southern Kingdom to rebel against the covenant (Hos 5:5; 7:10; 13:6; Jer 13:15–17). They failed to take God seriously and tried to fashion their lives according to their own rules and desires, and the result was the disaster of exile. In this they simply recapitulated the path blazed by Adam and Eve, who violated God's law, thinking they could be like gods unto themselves, and were exiled out of the land God had given them. In contrast to this, the proper approach to God is not just obedience, but obedience that flows from humility. This is why when exemplars of faithfulness like Abraham and Job approach God, they call themselves "dust and ashes," because before God and compared to God that's what they are (Gen 18:27; Job 42:6; also see Sir 10:9). In other words, because humility is the necessary way to understand the nature of humanity as created by God, complete humility is not just the prerequisite for approaching God, but it is what must characterize the nature of the ascent itself.

In the postexilic period the people of Israel were small in number, weak compared to the Persian Empire, frequently vulnerable to the strong and wicked, and many understood themselves to be in an ongoing theological state of exile. The way forward was to recognize this and take it to heart. The essential posture necessary for relating to God was the humility to place God back at the center of their individual and national lives. For the prophet Zephaniah, this would be the defining characteristic of God's people in the wake of the Babylonian exile:

> For then I [i.e., God] will remove from your
>   midst
>   the proud braggarts,
> And you shall no longer exalt yourself
>   on my holy mountain.

> But I will leave as a remnant in your midst
>   a people humble and lowly,
> who shall take refuge in the name of the LORD.
>   (Zeph 3:11–12)

Similarly, an anonymous prophet (or prophets) from the postexilic period called to the people with a message from God:

> This is the one whom I approve:
>   the afflicted one, crushed in spirit,
>   who trembles at my word. (Isa 66:2)

To those longing for God to return, forgive, and completely restore Israel, he reassured them:

> The spirit of the Lord GOD is upon me,
>   because the LORD has anointed me;
> He has sent me to bring good news to
>   the afflicted,
>   to bind up the brokenhearted,
> To proclaim liberty to the captives,
>   release to the prisoners. (Isa 61:1)

Central to the viability of faith and hope in the postexilic period was a humility that led one to worship and obey no matter the present circumstances. This is precisely what is advocated in the last group of psalms in the Psalms of Ascents. Psalms 130–31 complement each other in terms of the proper disposition for a worshiper of God and Psalms 132–33 complement each other regarding the mutual relational harmony between God and his servants (a vertical devotion) and between those within the people of God (a horizontal devotion). Psalm 134 then provides a kind of benediction for the life made whole in relation to both God and God's people. It is here that the humble pilgrim finally reaches the denouement of the literary journey.

PSALM 130: OUT OF THE DEPTHS

Since the time of the early Church, Psalm 130 has traditionally been numbered among the seven penitential psalms (the others are Pss 6, 32, 38, 51, 102, and 143). These psalms may be considered a subcategory of laments in which the Psalmist confesses guilt and the need for forgiveness. Not surprisingly, Augustine had a special appreciation for the penitential psalms and meditated on them constantly, including on his deathbed. Following Augustine, many others throughout the history of the Church have been drawn to these psalms as a poignant articulation of humanity's unworthiness before God. In Psalm 130, the Psalmist wrestles with an important tension in religious belief in achieving a balance between urgent, distressed anticipation and patient confidence in the grace of God.

PSALM 130

¹ A song of ascents.

Out of the depths I call to you, LORD;
  ² Lord, hear my cry!
May your ears be attentive
  to my cry for mercy.
³ If you, LORD, keep account of sins,
  Lord, who can stand?
⁴ But with you is forgiveness
  and so you are revered.

⁵ I wait for the Lᴏʀᴅ,
　my soul waits
　and I hope for his word.
⁶ My soul looks for the Lord
　more than sentinels for daybreak.
More than sentinels for daybreak,
　⁷ let Israel hope in the Lᴏʀᴅ,
For with the Lᴏʀᴅ is mercy,
　with him is plenteous redemption,
⁸ And he will redeem Israel
　from all its sins.

Psalm 130 is frequently known by its Latin title, *De Profundis,* "out of the depths," which translates just one word in Hebrew. This is unusual because normally laments flesh out the nature of the distress that is being faced. Here, though, the distress is expressed in a word that is both general yet evocative. As a general term, it allows people in a variety of situations to identify with the psalm, for all people share in the depths of the human condition. Whether the depths are the *feeling* of guilt or a distressing situation that is *due* to the Psalmist's guilt is not clear; the history of interpretation shows that it has been read both ways.

The word *depths* is evocative because it calls to mind the deep waters that appear in biblical texts as a symbol of chaos, of the world undone. For example, the same word is used in Isaiah 51:10 to describe the cosmic abyss that God overcame and subdued to bring order to the world. It is the antonym of the world's created goodness. What the Psalmist feels, whether due to a sinking sense of guilt or due to inescapable threats as a consequence of sin (or both), is an overwhelming sense that he is helpless and out of control. He is trapped; he has nowhere firm to stand; he has nothing within himself to pull himself out; his frantic desperation contrasts with the steady inevitability of his descent. The depths are a place of darkness, confusion, disorientation, and fear. To sink into the depths is to feel oneself utterly alone and sliding toward the realm of death itself. As a place of darkness, disorder, and chaos, it is a place that feels as far away from the presence of God as one can get. In this single Hebrew word, "out of the depths," the Psalmist gives voice to all those who have likewise felt the intense suffocation of sin or its consequences, the sense of drowning in a world being dismantled.

In such a place the Psalmist does the only thing still in his power to do: he calls out to God. His situation has at least made clear what was always true but often unseen, that for his very being he is wholly dependent on God, and not just as the one who can rescue him, but as the one who constitutes in himself the only basis on which the Psalmist might be rescued. Nothing within the Psalmist commends a deliverance. If deliverance is coming, it is not because of who he is, but because of who God is. Most especially, the Lord is the God who hears. False gods and idols notoriously fail to hear, do not care to hear, or are too distracted to hear. But Israel's God hears, in fact inclines his ear to hear. Like the outstretched deity of the Sistine Chapel, Israel's God strains to reach out to people even when they are drowning in the depths. As another Psalmist says, "If I ascend to the heavens, you are there; if I lie down in Sheol, there you are" (Ps 139:8). No cry is so distant or alienated that God is not eager to hear it.

God's eagerness to respond to cries from the depths of any abyss flows from who he is rather than what humans can offer to him. There is no attempt to divide humanity into "righteous" and "wicked," as in Psalm 1, or an attempt to compare himself favorably to others. All the Psalmist can offer is his cry of helplessness and the recognition that no one has a foothold to deserve deliverance from the depths. In contrast to the universal nature of humanity in verse 3, the Psalmist makes a claim about God's *nature* rather than makes a request for grace.

The tension that has been running through the first half of the psalm is whether the Psalmist's fate will be determined by the demands of God's justice or by God's merciful desire to restore. Justice and mercy are, of course, both central to God's character according to Scripture. The classic description of how they are related occurs when God renews the covenant after the golden calf incident. In Exodus 34 God passes before Moses and a description of his character is given in 34:6–7: "The LORD, the LORD, a God gracious and merciful, slow to anger and abounding in love and fidelity, continuing his love for a thousand generations, and forgiving wickedness, rebellion, and sin; yet not declaring the guilty guiltless, but bringing punishment for their parents' wickedness on children and children's children to the third and fourth generation!" This is the first of ten times in the Hebrew Bible God is described in this way (also see Num 14:18; Neh 9:17; Pss 86:15; 103:8; 145:8; Joel 2:13; Jonah 4:2; Mic 7:18; Nah 1:3); the key claim in this description is that while God is mysteriously both perfectly merciful and perfectly just, it is his mercy that has primacy. In alluding to Exodus 34 in Psalm 130:4 and 7, the Psalmist affirms the same theology. Because of his own character he has no reason to expect anything but just condemnation, but because of God's character he can hope for mercy.

Verse 4, in fact, represents the turning point of the psalm in which his descent into the depths is transformed into a spiritual ascent through hope. Even in the abyss he can worship (v. 4), wait (v. 5), and hope (v. 6). The awareness of divine grace is transformative; it reconstitutes the present in light of the listening, merciful God. To wait in this way is to orient the present toward what one knows through faith the future will be. The Psalmist waits for God's word, which will make all things right and render all things intelligible, even his own experience. Like the night sentinel, he may feel the darkness all around him and be unable to escape it on his own, but he knows the dawn is coming in God's own time and that in the meantime God is not as far away as he might seem. He is somehow mysteriously present with the Psalmist in his depths.

The hope of this solitary Psalmist transitions to the plight of all Israel in verses 7–8. His experience is not unique but becomes emblematic of Israel's story writ large. For God's mercy is demonstrated throughout sacred history in his plenteous acts of redemption from one dark depth after another. Even during the long night of Babylonian exile and then the Persian Empire, Israel's hope was not grounded in themselves, but in the character of God. Their sins had plunged them into the depths of despair. With the destruction of the temple, the loss of kingship, and the exile from their land, their world was dismantled and undone. It was easy to feel as though God was far away. Yet, because the Lord is a God who hears, they in turn could patiently listen for his word (v. 5); they could endure the darkness because the light was coming (v. 6). Because God is faithful, the light always does. For Israel, as for the Psalmist, the depths can never have the last word. The last word must always be *grace.*

PSALM 131: THE STILL, SMALL SOUL

Interpreters are almost universally enchanted by Psalm 131 because of its simplicity and air of serenity. They also frequently note the contrast between its brevity and its profundity. Although it is the second shortest psalm (after Ps 117), it is among the most challenging because it touches on an issue at the core of the human condition.

PSALM 131

¹ A song of ascents. Of David.

LORD, my heart is not proud;
   nor are my eyes haughty.
I do not busy myself with great matters,
   with things too sublime for me.
² Rather, I have stilled my soul,
Like a weaned child to its mother,
   weaned is my soul.
³ Israel, hope in the LORD,
   now and forever.

In the Hebrew of verse 1 there is a suggestive pun using the idea of height. This song of "ascent" begins by saying that the Psalmist's heart is not "elevated" nor are his eyes "lifted up." Both of these expressions are biblical idioms for arrogance (hence their translation as "proud" and "haughty" in the NABRE), but a more literal rendering brings out the paradox of Psalm 131: people must lower themselves if they wish to go up toward God. To ascend to Jerusalem and therefore to the presence of God requires that pilgrims humble themselves rather than exalt themselves. The difference between walking about with "raised eyes" and lifting one's eyes to the hills (Ps 121:1) is who stands as the object of the gaze, the self or God. Through the juxtaposition of heart and eyes, the Psalmist signals that his humility is both an internal characteristic of his attitude and will as well as the way he engages with the rest of the world.

The phrasing of the second half of verse 1 brings to mind especially the character of Job. Throughout Israel's history the Wisdom tradition had long recognized that there are things that God has set beyond the reach of human knowledge. In contemplating the mysterious movements of the world, an ancient sage had characterized some of them as "too wonderful for me" and beyond his understanding (Prov 30:18). Much later Ben Sira would warn his students not to seek after knowledge that is "too sublime" for them, but instead to remain humble in the face of the limits placed on humanity by God (Sir 3:20–22). It is in the Book of Job, though, where this concern takes center stage. In the face of inexplicable suffering and a world that seems wholly unfair, God's inscrutable nature is a running theme in the dialogues between Job and his friends (see Job 5:9; 9:10; 28:20–21; 37:5, 14). At the climactic moment of the book when God confronts Job in the whirlwind, Job confesses his inability to make sense of the world in words nearly the same in Hebrew as those at the end of Ps 131:1: "I have spoken but did not understand; things too marvelous for me, which I did not know" (Job 42:3). This recognition then moves Job to a docile acceptance of his state, which he characterizes in the evocative imagery of humility, "dust and ashes" (Job 42:6). While Job never receives an explanation for his suffering, he does receive a life-changing encounter with God that transforms how he understands himself and his place in the world.

Similarly, in Psalm 131 the fourfold expression of humility in verse 1 is not so much an expression of self-confidence by the Psalmist in the virtue of his own outlook as it is a confession of his own inadequacy to make sense of a world sometimes awash in confusion. In connection with Job, Psalm 131 very likely presupposes a backstory for the Psalmist of struggle, suffering, disappointment, and frustration. In a world marked by things humans cannot makes sense of and in which, like Job, an answer to the question "why?" may never come, to arrive at a place of humble acceptance rather than bitter resentment is no easy task; it requires long cultivation and a willingness to live indefinitely with the unresolved ambiguities of life.

The details of the backstory of struggle are left unstated, but the Psalmist alludes to it in verse 2 with the metaphor of weaning. The image of mother and weaned child admits of two possible comparisons. Some interpreters think the image is of a child resting with contentment on the mother after a feeding. On this reading, the point is that the Psalmist has reached the point of being content and nourished with whatever has been provided and not concerning himself with things he has not received. More likely, however, the image refers to the weaning from breastfeeding that occurred around two to three years of age (one of the only other places this form of the verb is used is in Isa 28:9, which refers to this important life event). If so, then the Psalmist is referring to a process of maturing in which the child no longer loves the mother primarily just for what the mother provides him. Now the child continually deepens in his relationship to his mother and reciprocates the mother's love because of who the mother is rather than just what she gives.

Because all human lives will pass through experiences that are unfair or incomprehensible, the challenge to preserve religious faith in the midst of them, and even if answers for why never come, is one that confronts everyone. For some people, experiences that seem devoid of meaning or purpose cannot be endured, and faith begins to erode. For others, like Job and this Psalmist, these experiences lead to a humility and stillness that opens up the possibility for a deeper, more mysterious, and even richer encounter with God.

As in Psalm 130, here also the experience of the individual in encountering something inherent in the human condition leads in verse 3 to a larger lesson for the whole people of Israel. In the sacred tradition they too had been compared to a child whose divine parent had carried them through the various experiences of wilderness and exile (Deut 1:31; Isa 46:3–4; Hos 11:3). In some instances, prophets had arisen to explain the covenantal significance of what they were experiencing, but sometimes only after the fact. Now in the Persian period, when some aspects of exile seemed to continue, they had to reckon once again with a world that often did not make sense. If their faith were based only on the expectation that God must provide in a certain way, then their faith would be prone to collapse. If, however, they could still their souls in humility and learn the kind of trust and contentment of a child who believes his mother cares for him even at a time when she withdraws the intimate nourishment of the breast, then they could be moved to hope and to see how God might be working among them in unforeseen ways. This hope will not be offered only on the condition that it be fulfilled on their expected timeline or in an expected way. It will, rather, trust in God's timing and God's ways, even if they appear beyond human understanding. The only kind of hope that can endure "now and forever" is one that flows out of humility before the Lord.

PSALM 132: MUTUAL DEVOTION

The shortest of the Psalms of Ascents is followed by the longest. They are linked, however, by the mention of David and by the close theological connection between humility and religious devotion. As the center of the final grouping

of psalms, Psalm 132 represents the theological climax of
the theology of Jerusalem in the Psalms of Ascents.

PSALM 132

¹ A song of ascents.

Remember, O LORD, for David
    all his hardships;
² How he swore an oath to the LORD,
    vowed to the Mighty One of Jacob:
³ "I will not enter the house where I live,
    nor lie on the couch where I sleep;
⁴ I will give my eyes no sleep,
    my eyelids no rest,
⁵ Till I find a place for the LORD,
    a dwelling for the Mighty One of Jacob."
⁶ "We have heard of it in Ephrathah;
    we have found it in the fields of Jaar.
⁷ Let us enter his dwelling;
    let us worship at his footstool."
⁸ "Arise, LORD, come to your resting place,
    you and your mighty ark.
⁹ Your priests will be clothed with justice;
    your devout will shout for joy."
¹⁰ For the sake of David your servant,
    do not reject your anointed.

¹¹ The LORD swore an oath to David in truth,
    he will never turn back from it:
"Your own offspring I will set upon your throne.
¹² If your sons observe my covenant,
    and my decrees I shall teach them,
Their sons, in turn,
    shall sit forever on your throne."
¹³ Yes, the LORD has chosen Zion,
    desired it for a dwelling:

14 "This is my resting place forever;
    here I will dwell, for I desire it.
15 I will bless Zion with provisions;
    its poor I will fill with bread.
16 I will clothe its priests with salvation;
    its devout shall shout for joy.
17 There I will make a horn sprout for David;
    I will set a lamp for my anointed.
18 His foes I will clothe with shame,
    but on him his crown shall shine."

Psalm 132 contemplates the complex relationship between David's devotion to God and God's devotion to both David and Jerusalem. It is one of several places in the Bible that describe God's promise to David, the best known of which is 2 Samuel 7. In that story, David had waited patiently on God's timing, refusing to raise his hand against Saul, who at the time was "the Lord's anointed," in a manner similar to the outlook of Psalm 131. After Saul's death, though, David was anointed king in Hebron (2 Sam 2) and consolidated his power over all twelve tribes of Israel (2 Sam 3 – 5). He conquered the city of Jerusalem, which was advantageously situated between his own power base in Bethlehem and that of Saul's family, and then he brought the ark there (2 Sam 6). Then David did what ancient Near Eastern kings typically did; he offered to build a temple for his God. God, however, responded that this was unnecessary; and instead of David's building a "house" for God (i.e., a temple), God would build a "house" (i.e., a dynasty) for David. If future kings from David's line would disobey, they would be punished, but God would not go back on his promise to David. And thus, the Davidic dynasty was born. It was bound up with God's choice of Zion and was considered to be equally unshakeable because it was grounded in God's faithfulness to his promises.

Commentators often characterize the promise in 2 Samuel 7 as "unconditional" and contrast it with Psalm 132, in which the promise seems more "conditional," that is, based on obedience. While this characterization can be helpful to a degree, it is also a bit misleading because the language of "unconditional" and "conditional" are *transactional* terms. The complex relationship between God and his chosen is better characterized as "covenantal," which is inherently personal and can therefore involve some aspects that are "unconditional" and others that are "conditional."[2] What Psalm 132 focuses on is the reciprocal devotion between God and David, even while highlighting an important asymmetry in that relationship.

For David's part, his devotion is characterized as an unwavering commitment to serve God even at great cost to himself. David's prioritization of God above all else is an exemplary illustration of the kind of humility pictured in Psalm 131 and is what sets him apart from Saul. In the crucial test of his kingship, Saul had feared the people more than God and so had disobeyed the divine command from Samuel. In deciding to hold back the best from the Amalekites instead of devoting it to destruction for God, Saul proved himself unworthy (1 Sam 15:22–24). Even though there were instances in which David also sinned egregiously, his distinctive characteristic was that he made the glory of God his priority and constantly deferred to God's will. This concern comes out clearly already in the battle with Goliath (1 Sam 17:45–46) and continues right up to his commitment to honor God with a temple even if it means

---

2. This point is emphasized by John Goldingay, *Psalms*, vol. 3, *Psalms 90—150*, Baker Commentary on the Old Testament (Grand Rapids: Baker Academic, 2008), 559–62.

depriving himself.[3] This is the instance Psalm 132 is high-lighting (in terms somewhat different from 2 Sam 7), but it is really the culmination of David's key character trait.

For God's part, Psalm 132 makes an important theological move that can be easy to overlook. The choice of David is interconnected with God's choice of Jerusalem, but because God's choice of both preceded the building of the temple by Solomon, it follows that it remained in force even after the temple had been destroyed by the Babylonians. Further, God's choice of Jerusalem was rooted in his desire for the place as the location from which he could pour out blessing (vv. 13–16). The language used by the Psalmist in verses 13–14 suggests that God had not just selected Zion but had fallen in love with it as the place where he could dwell among his people. Ultimately, the flourishing of provision, salvation, and joy are from the initiative of God's love rather than from human merit. As such, God's choice of Jerusalem does not have the same contingency as the continuation of the royal line does. Yet, even with the royal line, punishment is not the final word but only an abeyance. For, verses 17–18 envision a future for David's line as well. Even though David's descendants broke the covenant and precipitated the exile, God's faithfulness to David means that he will eventually restore the Davidic line.

What would Psalm 132 have meant to those living in the Persian period when there was no Davidic king on the throne? First, by focusing on the time when God himself came to Jerusalem in the procession of the ark of the covenant (vv. 6–9), the psalm encourages pilgrims to

---

3. This reading of the David story is indebted to Claire Mathews McGinnis, "Swimming with the Divine Tide: An Ignatian Reading of 1 Samuel," in *Theological Exegesis: Essays in Honor of Brevard S. Childs*, ed. Christopher Seitz and Kathryn Greene-McCreight (Grand Rapids: Eerdmans, 1998), 240–70.

see their own journey to Jerusalem as retracing that initial "pilgrimage" David made with God. God is not only found in Jerusalem; he is found within the journey as well. Second, for those with eyes to see, God's presence can be found even in everyday realities such as the feeding of the poor, striving for justice, and the joy of the devout (vv. 9, 15–16). Third, a present that is faithful must be shaped by the memory of the past and a hope for the future; indeed, it becomes an embodied living out of this memory and hope. Each pilgrimage derives its deeper meaning from the way it resonates and transforms the liturgical movements of the past and anticipates the fuller blessings of God's presence among the people in the future. In a time when the ark had been lost during the exile and the house of David had fallen, when the priests were not always agents of justice and the devout did not always shout for joy, the Psalmist could at least take solace in the fact that their destiny wholly depended on God's faithfulness to his promises and his desire to bless Jerusalem. Once that is grasped, it becomes possible, like David, to seek the Lord with humility and openness, no matter the present cost or what the immediate future may bring.

PSALM 133: UNITY FLOWS DOWN

In the Psalms of Ascents, Psalm 133 is the last psalm before the benediction in Psalm 134 and presents a stark contrast with the conflict and antagonism described in Psalm 120 at the beginning of the collection. Viewed together, these psalms show that an integral part of the pilgrimage journey should be the communal movement from fragmentation to unity.

PSALM 133

¹ A song of ascents. Of David.

How good and how pleasant it is,
    when brothers dwell together as one!
² Like fine oil on the head,
    running down upon the beard,
Upon the beard of Aaron,
    upon the collar of his robe.
³ Like dew of Hermon coming down
    upon the mountains of Zion.
There the Lᴏʀᴅ has decreed a blessing,
    life for evermore!

According to the biblical narrative, life outside of Eden has been marred from the very beginning by the inability of brothers to live in peace, much less unity. In the first story after Adam and Eve were exiled from Eden, Cain is overcome with jealousy because of God's choice of Abel and so he slays his brother. The pattern of rivalry, jealousy, and murderous intent among brothers is played out over and over again in later generations as well. Jacob swindles the birthright and blessing from his brother Esau and then must flee to escape Esau's murderous anger. Joseph flaunts his favored status, and his brothers throw him in a pit before selling him into slavery in Egypt. When the Israelites (the descendants of Jacob) are freed from slavery in Egypt, the Edomites (the descendants of Esau) oppose and hassle them (Num 20:14–21). After experiencing some unity under David and Solomon, the tribes of Israel (the descendants of Joseph and his brothers) fracture into a Northern Kingdom and a Southern Kingdom. According to Ezra–Nehemiah, after the exile there was conflict between those returning

90

from Babylon and those already in the land, between those in Judea and those in Samaria, and between different factions within Jerusalem. Brotherly conflict has been a running theme throughout sacred history, and in that history, it is evident that division and exile, conflict and alienation, are never far apart. Each one typically leads to the other. Conversely, Ezekiel signaled that restoration from exile and unity also go hand in hand when he took two sticks, representing the Northern and Southern Kingdoms, and bound them together to demonstrate the unification that would accompany restoration (Ezek 37:15–27). True unity among God's people, then, became an essential feature of the eschatological ideal.

Set over against the historical reality of discord, Psalm 133 extols the essential goodness and desirability of unity among God's people through two vivid comparisons. The first image is of oil running down the beard of the inaugural high priest, Aaron. Pouring out oil signaled hospitality, joy, and sensory pleasure. The amount poured out for this anointing suggests expensive lavishness, an abundance that flows down the beard and even onto the garments of the high priest. Significantly, the high priest's vestments were adorned with jewels that symbolically represented the unity of the tribes of Israel. The second image is of the dew of Hermon coming down on the mountains of Zion. Geographically this would be impossible since Hermon was a mountain well north of Jerusalem, but the image is a poetic and theological claim rather than a literal one. Although the area around Jerusalem could be quite arid, Mount Hermon was famous for its dew. In fact, its snow-capped mountains often supplemented the falling dew, creating an abundance of refreshing water. To picture this as flowing to Zion is to give an image of life-giving water from heaven. In other words, in the parched landscape of communal conflict, the dual images of the oil of anointing and the dew of heaven suggest lavish and life-giving refreshment.

Against the pattern of nearly constant human conflict it would be tempting to see Psalm 133 as unrealistic, but it is no facile hope in which people are naively encouraged just to get along; it is rather an ideal to strive for and an iconic image of what the ultimate restoration of God's people will look like. In the meantime, however, the pilgrimage festivals offered an imperfect embodiment of this anticipated reality. On a recurring schedule, the whole people would be called to assemble together in Jerusalem to celebrate God's acts of redemption that forged the identity of Israel as a people. In these liturgical rhythms a picture of the people united in worship with God at the center could be glimpsed. Yet until the eschatological actualization of unity, any provisional unity will remain fragile and temporary. The ending of Psalm 133 suggests that like oil descending on the high priest and the dew of heaven descending on Mount Zion, unity will only be possible as a blessing that flows down from God. Further, the placement of Psalm 133 near the end of the Psalms of Ascents is appropriate insofar as it suggests that real and abiding unity is only feasible in a community that is characterized by patterns of repentance (Ps 130), humility (Ps 131), and devotion to both God and one another (Ps 132).

PSALM 134: BENEDICTION

In this short closing benediction to the Psalms of Ascents, the Psalmist brings to a crescendo the themes of praise, unity, reciprocal blessing, worship, and the centrality of God's presence in Zion. It may have served as an actual liturgical piece for use at the temple, or it may have been composed (or perhaps extracted from a larger hymn) explicitly to serve as the literary conclusion to the whole Psalms of Ascents.

PSALM 134

¹ A song of ascents.

O come, bless the LORD,
　all you servants of the LORD
You who stand in the house of the LORD
　throughout the nights.
² Lift up your hands toward the sanctuary,
　and bless the LORD.
³ May the LORD bless you from Zion,
　the Maker of heaven and earth.

Pilgrimages had as their goal an encounter with the God of Zion in the temple of Jerusalem, and with this closing psalm the pilgrims are there and are summoned to worship. Here in the temple they image the unity of Psalm 133 in their communal act of worship. Here they join with the priests, both in voice and body, to extol the goodness of their God. It is surely significant that the addressees of this psalm are both the plural "you" in verses 1–2 and a singular "you" in verse 3. Individual worshipers are not lost in community but find their place within it.

This worship is structured by rhythms. Temporally, the worship spans the oscillations between days and nights. In Psalm 130 the night evoked a sense of anxiety and anticipation; here the night can be the occasion of communion with God. Through the revolutions of time, the worship of God goes on. There is also a rhythm of vertical space. As the people on earth direct their worship toward the God of heaven who is found in the temple, their God responds with blessing toward them from Zion, the unique meeting place of heaven and earth. Worship, praise, and blessing flow back and forth through this mutual devotion. And finally, there is a rhythm of horizontal space. As the pilgrims travel back home, they take the blessing of God with them to be realized in the ordinariness of their lives. Even as they depart Zion, they know that the liturgy will go on and in future years during the pilgrimage festivals they might return and repeat the same liturgy again. In its consistent patterns but ever new expressions, the liturgies of worship will structure and shape their lives. And so, Psalm 134 is a fitting end to the Psalms of Ascents. Literarily, it is the doxological finale of the collection, but it is also a summons, an invocation, for how the rest of life should be lived. Having ascended to Zion to bless the God of Israel, the pilgrims are now sent back out bearing the blessing of their God along their journey of life.

CONCLUSION

Psalms 130–34 are best understood in relation to one another and, as a group, as the apotheosis of the Psalms of Ascents. The pairing of Psalms 130 and 131 highlights the deep connection between repentance and humility. In following Psalms 120–29, they also make clear that threats to spiritual progression are not always external; there is normally an internal struggle as well. In many ways, these can be the struggles that are the hardest to confront and to overcome because they require releasing control, recognizing inadequacy, and accepting limitations. Yet, as many of the Church fathers recognized, without overcoming pride it is impossible to show the kind of unwavering devotion to

God described in Psalm 132. Without humility there can be no communal harmony as in Psalm 133.

And so despite his greatness in many respects, the figure of David functions as the paradigmatic pilgrim in these psalms. He is the one who first brought the ark of the covenant, and therefore divine worship, to Jerusalem. Yet, at a deeper level, he embodied the kind of selfless humility that should characterize all pilgrims as they gather as one community to worship. To place God at the center of one's life and devotion means a willingness, even eagerness, to exalt God even at great personal cost. As such, this final set of five psalms brings to the fore a number of paradoxes. In order to ascend, the pilgrims must lower themselves. To find communal unity, they must decenter themselves. To find wholeness, they must lose themselves in the centrality of the worship of God. And when this orientation characterizes their journey, the pilgrims will lift their eyes only to find blessing coming down.

CHAPTER 5

The Psalms of Ascents as Christian Scripture

From Homer's *Odyssey* to Dante's *Divine Comedy* to J. R. R. Tolkien's *The Lord of the Rings*, there is something enthralling to humans about journeys, especially those in which the outward journey is matched by an inward journey. Journeys assume that things are not as they should be, but also that change and progress are possible. They are launched by the blend of desire and hope as they seek transformation. Such a dynamic that resonates in certain respects with the experience of those who composed the Psalms of Ascents (especially Pss 120, 124, and 129) is eloquently captured in Dorothy Sayers's description of Dante's motivation in writing the *Divine Comedy*:

> This was the task which Dante had set for himself... in the wreck of all his earthly hopes. He had lost love and youth and earthly goods and household peace and citizenship and active political usefulness and the dream of a decent world and a reign of justice. He was stripped bare. He looked outward upon the corruption of Church and Empire, and he looked inward into the corruption of the human heart; and what he saw was the vision of Hell. And, having seen it, he set himself down to

write the great Comedy of Redemption and of the return of all things by the Way of Self-Knowledge and Purification, to the beatitude of the Presence of God.[1]

Similarly, out of their own experiences of conflict, injustice, and pain, the authors of the Psalms of Ascents articulate a hopeful vision of the spiritual life that is rooted in the quest for God's transforming presence in Zion.

In chapters 2–4 we have traced the theology of the Psalms of Ascents, both as arising from a context of actual pilgrimage journeys and as constituting a literary work that enables any reader to "journey" through them. In this chapter we explore how this collection may fruitfully function in a Christian canonical context in which the goal and summit of interpretation is the revelation of God in Christ.

THE PSALMS OF ASCENTS AND THE THEOLOGY OF PILGRIMAGE

As a collection, the Psalms of Ascents were crafted in a time of uncertainty when those in Jerusalem were rethinking and transforming the sacred tradition in light of the Babylonian exile and their new reality as part of the Persian Empire. As such, this "miniature psalter" shows some continuity with the worship and theology of the preexilic period, but also a flexibility in adapting this theology to bring hope in their current circumstances.

The conviction that the past provides the theological resources to understand the present and to project

---

1. Dante Alighieri, *The Divine Comedy*, 1: *Hell*, trans. Dorothy Sayers (Harmondsworth: Penguin Books, 1949), 48–49.

the possibilities for the future flows out of Israel's understanding of time. Often biblical authors are said to have a "linear" view of time, in contrast to a "circular" view of time. In one sense this is true in that salvation history progresses from creation at the beginning to consummation at the end. But in another sense, this is not quite adequate because in ancient Judaism time was structured with repeating patterns. In terms of the calendar, time was structured each week by the Sabbath, each year by the festivals, each set of years by the sabbatical year, and so forth. The pilgrimage festivals obviously participate in this calendrical cycle in celebrating God's great acts of redemption on a regular, yearly basis.

But even beyond these regular calendrical rhythms, there are redemptive historical themes that are understood to repeat, though not at regular intervals and not in exactly the same way. Periods of exile, captivity, and oppression from the past are used to render intelligible new experiences of these realities. Likewise, redemptive acts such as the exodus function as types for understanding other acts of redemption, including those hoped for in the future. This means that while in one sense Israel's history is linear, there are also interlocking patterns of repetition as well, which creates a spiral-like pattern. With each revolution around the spiral there is both a "closeness" to earlier places on the spiral, but also a newness from being farther along. A key part of the theology of the Psalms of Ascents is based on this spiral-like nature of salvation history.

For example, the figures of David and Solomon are prominent in the Psalms of Ascents. David appears in the superscriptions of Psalms 122, 124, 131, and 133, and as the subject of Psalm 132. The accent is not on David as military conqueror or even as the one who seized Jerusalem in particular. Rather, David functions more as the paradigm of pilgrimage, as an ideal type of the devoted pilgrim. He is the one who rejoiced to go to Jerusalem to worship (Ps 122), the one who recognizes that salvation and survival are due to God's grace (Ps 124), who exemplifies humility (Ps 131), and prizes harmony among God's people (Ps 133). At root, he is someone who embodies a self-sacrificial devotion to God (Ps 132). Solomon is less prominent, but he appears in the superscription of the central psalm in the whole collection (Ps 127). As the builder of the first temple and the paradigmatic sage, he facilitates a theological connection that is drawn between the goodness of an ordinary family living an ordinary life in the fear of the LORD and the whole people gathered as the family of God at the house of God in Jerusalem. It is hardly a coincidence that for some biblical authors during the Persian period (e.g., the author of Chronicles) these two kings represented the glory days of Israel when all twelve tribes were united and when Jerusalem gained its theological significance. The Psalms of Ascents advocates a manner of living defined by wisdom and obedience even when life seems not to make much sense. The collection of these psalms drives toward the assembling before God of all of God's people in peace, unity, and worship of the ever-faithful covenantal God of Israel.

Another way the spiral-like quality of sacred history can be seen in these psalms is through the use of the categories of exile and restoration to make sense of Israel's recent history in Babylon and in the Persian period. The clearest instance of this is in Psalm 126, where the Psalmist assumes the postexilic situation is analogous to the Babylonian exile and therefore that the partial restoration that came about under Cyrus can produce a hope that eventually God will bring full and final restoration as well. The patterns of exile and restoration indicate not divine apathy or abandonment, but the unshakeable faithfulness of God to redeem Israel over and over again. By situating present afflictions and frustrations within this repeating pattern, the faithful are able to see a deeper reality at work. They can defer to God's timing and God's ways, even when these do not seem to make sense or seem to confound expectations. And in the meantime, they do not wait passively for redemption to come, but actively seek the good of Jerusalem and her people (Ps 122). The iconic portrayals of a city restored and a people healed reshape the worshiper's perspective on the present by viewing it in light of the eschatological future.

Key to this theology of the Psalms of Ascents is the centrality and supremacy of Israel's God. God is presented as the one on whom Israel is totally dependent and the one who is the singular source of Israel's hope. Further, it is because of God's choice of Jerusalem as the place in which his presence can be encountered that gives Jerusalem its importance as the "center" of the world. The significance of Jerusalem is derivative of God's gracious desire to dwell among his chosen people. While in the Psalms of Ascents Jerusalem remains the place of joy, peace, unity, and the locus of God's presence, this importance is now more a function of the covenantal relationship between God and Israel than of any inherent, mythic quality of Jerusalem itself. The earlier motif of Zion's invincibility has been rethought in light of the deeper reality of God's unshakeable commitment to Israel. The only faith that can be unshakeable is the one that is grounded in the character of God rather than in the protection of ramparts and walls.

The understanding of salvation history as having a "spiral" quality is the basis of theological typology and means that when the early Christians read the Old Testament christologically, they were extending, albeit in new and surprising ways, the kind of organic theological development in which the authors of the Old Testament themselves had engaged.

To return to the image of Irenaeus discussed in chapter 1, how do these "tiles" from Psalms 120−34 fit into the mosaic of the revelation of God in Jesus Christ? Taking our cue from how the New Testament portrays Jesus as the culmination of the Old Testament story, we may suggest four ways that the pilgrimage theology of the Psalms of Ascents can contribute to the theological vision of the whole Christian canon.

JESUS AS THE ARCHETYPAL PILGRIM

When the New Testament refers to Jesus as the "son of David" it primarily has in view his messianic role as the king of Israel who is establishing the kingdom of God. In proclaiming that Jesus was restoring the Davidic kingdom, the New Testament authors were assuming that the state of exile (in the theological sense) that had continued into the Persian period also continued down to their own day. Think, for example, of the words of the Christmas carol "O Come, O Come Emmanuel," which describes "captive Israel" that "mourns in lonely exile here, until the Son of God appear."[2] The idea is that, despite being in the land with a temple, at the time of Jesus Israel remained in exile in some profound way and looked for the fulfillment of the promises of prophets like Isaiah and Ezekiel to signal their restoration: a new exodus that would usher in the reign of a new Davidic king over a renewed people of God worshiping in a new and glorious temple. It is not surprising, then, that throughout the Gospels, the royal role of Jesus is often coordinated with the coming to Jerusalem at the time of the pilgrimage

---

2. My thanks to Gary Anderson for bringing these lyrics to my attention.

festivals, especially Passover, which celebrated the exodus from Egypt and the journey to the promised land. When he enters Jerusalem on Palm Sunday, he is acclaimed the "son of David" (Matt 21:9), and then his passion unfolds at the time of the Passover. The new exodus and the new kingdom are of a piece.

Yet, in his final and most consequential journey to Jerusalem, Jesus brings the Psalms' theology of pilgrimage to a climax, but with some surprising twists. According to Luke, when Jesus arrives in Jerusalem, he finds it distressingly failing to be what it should. "As he drew near, he saw the city and wept over it, saying, 'If this day you only knew what makes for peace—but now it is hidden from your eyes'" (Luke 19:41–42). As he goes on teaching about Jerusalem's calling to peace and prayer, the hostility toward him only grows. He finds not peace, but conflict; not unity, but division; not blessing, but animosity; and so he laments rather than rejoices. He sows in tears (Ps 126:5–6), hoping for a later harvest of joy (Heb 12:2).

Rather than condemning and discarding Israel, he embodies Israel, taking on himself their history and their destiny. Israel's story becomes the template for his story. He is the one who feels hemmed in on all sides by those who desire his destruction (Ps 120). He is the one who is sated with mockery and contempt but keeps his eyes on the LORD (Ps 123). He is the one who commits himself totally to the hands of the LORD (Ps 121). He is the one who wills the good of Jerusalem even as they reject him (Ps 122). He is the one whom God vindicated when all others had risen against him (Ps 124). He is the one who trusts in the LORD even when injustice temporarily has the upper hand (Ps 125). He is the one who recapitulates the story of Israel in being viciously attacked, but ultimately delivered by the God who overcomes the forces of chaos and death (Ps 129).

He is the one who enters the depths of the human condition and waits on the LORD, not because of his own sin but in solidarity with others, utterly confident that God is profoundly merciful (Ps 130). He is the one who humbles himself (Ps 131) and is, like his ancestor David, devoted to the glory of God even at great cost to himself (Ps 132). And in this, he exemplifies the most important characteristics of the faithful Jewish pilgrim: humility and self-sacrificial devotion; in his suffering he appears to be defeated, but in reality he is bringing the kingdom. Or as Paul put it:

> Though he was in the form of God,
>> he did not regard equality with God
>>> something to be grasped.
>> Rather he emptied himself,
>> taking the form of a slave,
>> coming in human likeness;
>> and found in human appearance,
>> he humbled himself,
>>> becoming obedient to death,
>>> even death on a cross. (Phil 2:6–8)

However, in line with this passage from Philippians, the most unexpected twist is that Jesus not only exemplified the faithful Jewish pilgrim's journey to Jerusalem, but also embodied the journey *of God* back to Zion as well. Already in the Old Testament there was a sense that pilgrimages recapitulated God's journey from Sinai to Zion, culminating in David's bringing the ark to Jerusalem. But beginning with the Babylonian exile there was a sense that the restoration would be marked by God's returning to Jerusalem to dwell among his people. Isaiah 40 had described the return from exile as being heralded by a messenger who would announce the return of the LORD (Isa 40:3), and the Gospel of

Mark identifies this herald as John the Baptist (Mark 1:1–8). This implies that in some way Jesus represents the return of God to dwell among Israel, but it is unexpectedly a divine pilgrimage into human flesh.

The additional surprise, though, is that Jesus does not represent God's return in the form of conquest over Israel's enemies, but through the absorption of their hatred and violence. Because Jesus is both the archetypal pilgrim but also the coming of God, his own journey to Jerusalem is not so much to encounter God, as to manifest the presence of God. Jesus ascends to Jerusalem, indeed ascends to his climactic place on the cross, in order to descend into the depths of the human condition and thus unveil God's unshakeable, covenant commitment to dwell among his people. As one modern theologian puts it, "If God's 'exaltation' above the heavens manifests his 'glory,' then his 'glance into the depths' manifests his grace."[3] But we can go further: it is precisely in his self-sacrificing devotion that Jesus demonstrates not just grace, but the glory of who God is. He is the God who, at great cost to himself, journeys to meet humanity and enters our abyss with us and for us. As we fix our eyes on Christ crucified in Jerusalem, we behold the identity and presence of God in a way that no previous pilgrims could.

THE INCARNATION AND THE RECENTERING OF SACRED SPACE

At the heart of the New Testament faith is the conviction that in Jesus, God has come to dwell among humanity

---

3.   Hans Urs von Balthasar, *The Glory of the Lord*, vol. 6: *Theology: The Old Covenant*, trans. Brian McNeil and Erasmo Leiva-Merkakis (Edinburgh: T&T Clark, 1991), 69.

in a mode of unprecedented intimacy, namely the mystery of the incarnation. The Gospel of John articulates the significance of the incarnation as the culmination of temple theology. Jesus is the Word become flesh, tabernacling among Israel (John 1:14). The presence of God that could be found in the Jerusalem temple was now incomprehensibly, immeasurably intensified in the person of Jesus Christ. While this "incarnational" recentering of temple theology was unexpected, it was not completely unprecedented. Already in the Psalms of Ascents there was a tendency to see the location of God's presence in Jerusalem as having more to do with its role as the center of the chosen people than any mythic quality. Even the physical structures are described in almost communal terms, as in 122:3. But even more to the point, the old Zion imagery of security is now reapplied to those with faith (125:1). An analogy is drawn between the security afforded Jerusalem by the mountains and that afforded the people by the LORD (125:2). A further important feature of this understanding of Israel is the tendency among the Psalms of Ascents to portray the experience of the singular Psalmist (or the figure of David) as a type for the larger salvation historical experience of the whole people. There are hints of this throughout Psalms 120—34, but it is especially prominent in the final five psalms.

Importantly, the significance of Jerusalem is not set aside (pilgrimage still occurs, after all), but it is reconfigured in relation to the *people among whom God dwells*. As Erich Zenger explains, "Jerusalem is indeed the center of the world, in the view of the Pilgrim Psalter, but it is not a cosmic center; rather, it is the center of Israel with a centripetal and centrifugal power to bless."[4] In other words, in the view of the Psalms of Ascents, Jerusalem is the primary

---

4. Frank-Lothar Hossfeld and Erich Zenger, *Psalms 3: A Commentary on Psalms 101—150*, trans. Linda M. Maloney (Minneapolis: Fortress Press, 2011), 297.

place to encounter God's blessing, but as a launching place from which blessing flows out to all of Israel, wherever and whoever they are. In fact, a notable feature of the Psalms of Ascents is how seriously it takes the importance of everyday lives. In these psalms, God is both interested and involved in the ordinary lives of Israelites, even if they live far away from Jerusalem. Blessing is available not just to those who operate the levers of power in Jerusalem, but even to the ordinary, the unnamed, the overlooked, and the afflicted. The sacred centrality of Jerusalem is not one that excludes and marginalizes those outside it, but one that envelops and transforms those who seek it.

New Testament authors portray Jesus as not just an Israelite, but as the paradigmatic Israelite who represents, embodies, and lives out the story of the whole people. This is why, for example, Matthew is careful to show how Jesus recapitulates the major events in Israel's history such as his baptism (the crossing of the Red Sea), his temptation for forty days in the wilderness (the forty years in the desert), the Sermon on the Mount (receiving the covenant at Sinai), and so on. From this angle, the tendency in the Psalms of Ascents to associate the presence of God in Jerusalem with the dwelling of God among all of Israel may be seen as a type, an anticipation, of the more radical indwelling of God among Israel in the singular and representative person of Jesus, the archetypal Israelite. And from this person blessing flows out, not just to Israel but to the whole world.

Yet, does the recentering of sacred space in the person of Jesus mean there is no continuing role in Christianity for Jerusalem? Here the answer is complex. On one hand, Jerusalem (and pilgrimage toward it) are significantly relativized. New Testament authors recast the pilgrimage to Jerusalem in spiritual terms as a journey toward the heavenly Jerusalem. For example, the author of Hebrews says,

"You have approached Mount Zion and the city of the living God, the heavenly Jerusalem, and countless angels in festal gathering, and the assembly of the firstborn enrolled in heaven, and God the judge of all" (Heb 12:22–23). Among other New Testament authors, the imagery of the temple and of its priesthood is applied not just to Christ, but to the Church as the Body of Christ (see 1 Pet 2:1–10).

On the other hand, Jerusalem does still play a significant role in the New Testament; it is still not quite like just any other city. The first council is held there to decide how to handle Gentile converts and the leaders there are held in special esteem (Acts 15). Even throughout his missionary efforts among the Gentiles, Paul considers it important for his churches to send donations to the church in Jerusalem (Acts 11:27–30; 2 Cor 8–9). It is also surely theologically significant that the Church holds that redemption was accomplished in an actual physical body in an actual physical space. Particular spaces as possible bearers of sacredness still matter. Yet, the idea of Christians making pilgrimage to Jerusalem grew rather slowly over the next several centuries. Even today when Christians make a pilgrimage to Jerusalem, it is not for the usual reasons people make religious pilgrimages. Upon entering the Church of the Holy Sepulchre, pilgrims stand in line to enter the edicule, which marks the spot where Jesus is thought to have been laid. Yet, upon entering this small space, one cannot help but be struck that what makes it sacred is not what is there, but what is *absent*. Unlike pilgrimages to the graves of saints and martyrs, in the edicule it is the absence of the body that makes that space what it is. The recentering of sacred space in the person of Jesus is utterly transformed by the resurrection because it means all space has the potential to be sanctified, to be a focal point of the overwhelming presence of God. The blessing of the God of Zion can be directly accessible *wherever* the risen Christ is present, whether in Jerusalem or elsewhere.

THE TRANSFORMATION OF SACRED TIME

As with sacred space, sacred time is also dramatically transformed through the coming of Christ as the incarnation of God. Already in the Old Testament, a hallmark of Zion theology was that Jerusalem was unique not just spatially (as the meeting place of heaven and earth), but also temporally. To worship in the temple at a given point in time is simultaneously to partake, in some way, of primordial and eschatological time. To be in Zion during sacred time (Sabbath, festivals, etc.) is to enter the world as it once was, should be, and will be again one day.[5] To return to the illustration of time as having a spiral-like quality, when one has traveled around one revolution of the coil, the path traced out is equal to the length of the circumference of the coil; however, one has ended up in a place adjacent to where one started. Similarly, points of sacred time such as the yearly festivals "touch" one another every time the calendar is cycled, making each instance of its celebration both new, but also intimately connected with previous and future points in sacred time, from creation to consummation.

Not surprisingly, this sense of time is a theme throughout the pilgrimage theology of the Psalms of Ascents. Moments of exile, oppression, and suffering "touch" one another on the "spiral" of time, as do moments of deliverance and restoration. The immediacy of these places on

---

5. On this point see Jon D. Levenson, *Sinai and Zion: An Entry into the Jewish Bible* (San Francisco: Harper & Row, 1985), 127–37.

the "spiral" of time is what makes the typological connections between them so potent and allows the pilgrims to lift their eyes beyond their immediate circumstances to see the larger divine patterns at work. Instead of becoming overwhelmed by their immediate circumstances in the Persian period, the faith expressed by these Psalmists has learned to see beyond the appearances of the present to behold a reality in which God is faithful and in control. Praying for peace and working for peace are not a naïve refusal to face reality nor a quixotic hope against hope. They are the natural results of an understanding of the covenantal nature of God's relationship to Israel and the interconnected aspects of sacred history.

According to the Apostle Paul, the coming of Christ has had a dramatic effect on what we have been describing as the spiral-like nature of time. The death and resurrection of Jesus have caused the spiral to be compressed so that the beginning and end of the human story can be seen all together in the middle of time (1 Cor 7:29).[6] This means that the concept of sacred time found in pilgrimage psalms has been greatly amplified and intensified in the time between the first and second comings of Christ. As Paul Griffiths describes the Apostle Paul's point, "The crucifixion, resurrection, and ascension of Jesus lie at the heart of time. That time is contracted by those events, pleated and folded around them, gathered by them into a tensely dense possibility; it has folds or gatherings in it because of its contraction."[7] The compression of the spiral due to the crucifixion and resurrection means that the present time can experience elements of eschatological time in a way not

---

6.   The NABRE translates this part of the verse as "time is running out," but the Greek has more the sense of contraction or compression rather than abbreviation.

7.   Paul J. Griffiths, *Decreation: The Last Things of All Creatures* (Waco, TX: Baylor University Press, 2014), 96.

quite possible before. The hope for peace, justice, unity, joy, restoration, indeed redemption longed for in the Psalms of Ascents has been brought from the eschaton into the present through the pilgrimage of God into human flesh.

LITURGY AND THE NATURE OF SPIRITUAL PILGRIMAGE

In the Old Testament, sacred space and sacred time came together in the celebrations of the Sabbath and the pilgrimage festivals in Jerusalem. In Christianity, the transformation of sacred space in the incarnation and the transformation of sacred time in the crucifixion and resurrection have transposed and intensified that reality in the eucharistic liturgy. The Church's liturgical life is both repetitive and ongoing; in other words, it too has a spiral-like quality. And at the center of the liturgy is the presence of Christ in the Eucharist, connecting the events of any space and any time where it is celebrated with the redemption accomplished at the center of history. But, further, as Paul Griffiths points out, as an anticipation of heaven, the liturgy also brings into the present space and time the reality of eternity. Liturgy, therefore, can be a means of healing through its spiral-like participation in the death and resurrection of Christ and, indeed the very life of God.[8]

In chapter 1, it was noted that the spirituality of the Psalms of Ascents is "sacramental" in that the physical journey is not just the means to encounter God but is part of the transformative process itself. Even while at home the

---

8. Griffiths, *Decreation*, 95–108. For the implications regarding the real presence of Christ in the Eucharist, see also his *Regret: A Theology* (Notre Dame, IN: University of Notre Dame Press, 2021), 33–52, esp. 38–40.

pilgrims rejoice (Ps 122:1) and as they travel toward Jerusalem their perspective is altered (Ps 121:1-2). Even after they depart Jerusalem, the LORD's blessing goes with them (Ps 121:8), for they know the worship of God goes on (Ps 134:1-3). The worship envisioned in the Psalms of Ascents is centered on God's presence in Jerusalem, but it also draws into it not only those who are currently worshiping in Jerusalem, but all those who humbly place God at the center of their lives. In setting the worshiper in a covenantal rather than transactional relationship to God, they endow the ordinary with the possibility of bearing the graciousness and blessing of God. In the new covenant the pilgrim Church journeys to the heavenly Jerusalem, continually shaped by the rhythmic repetitions of the liturgy. But such an upward pilgrimage is possible only because God himself journeyed into the depths of the human condition and transformed forever what it means to say that God dwells among his people.

Select Bibliography for Further Reading

Bartholomew, Craig, and Fred Hughes, eds. *Explorations in a Christian Theology of Pilgrimage*. Burlington, VT: Ashgate, 2004.

Brueggemann, Walter. *Spirituality of the Psalms*. Minneapolis: Fortress Press, 2002.

Clifford, Richard J. *Psalms 73 – 150*. Abingdon Old Testament Commentaries. Nashville: Abingdon Press, 2003.

Endres, John, and Julia D. E. Prinz. "Psalms." In *The Paulist Biblical Commentary*, edited by José Enrique Aguilar Chiu et al., 463–520. Mahwah, NJ: Paulist Press, 2018.

Gillingham, Susan. *Psalms through the Centuries*. Vol. 1. Oxford: Blackwell, 2008.

Goldingay, John. *Psalms*. Vol. 3, *Psalms 90 – 150*. Baker Commentary on the Old Testament. Grand Rapids: Baker Academic, 2008.

Grabbe, Lester L. *A History of the Jews and Judaism in the Second Temple Period*. Vol. 1, *Yehud: A History of the Persian Province of Judah*. Library of Second Temple Studies 47. New York: T&T Clark, 2004.

Hossfeld, Frank-Lothar, and Erich Zenger. *Psalms 3: A Commentary on Psalms 101 – 150*. Translated by Linda M. Maloney. Minneapolis: Fortress Press, 2011.

Knowles, Melody D. *Centrality Practiced: Jerusalem in the Religious Practice of Yehud and the Diaspora in the Persian*

Period. Archaeology and Biblical Studies 16. Atlanta: Society of Biblical Literature, 2006.

Levenson, Jon D. *Sinai and Zion: An Entry into the Jewish Bible*. San Francisco: Harper & Row, 1985.

Mays, James L. *Psalms*. Interpretation. Louisville, KY: Westminster John Knox, 1994.

McCann, J. Clinton, Jr. "Psalms." In *The New Interpreter's Bible*, vol. 6, 639–1280, edited by Leander E. Keck. Nashville: Abingdon Press, 1996.

Mowinckel, Sigmund. *The Psalms in Israel's Worship*. Translated by D. R. Ap-Thomas. Grand Rapids: Eerdmans, 2004. First published in 1962 by Blackwell (Oxford).

Sarna, Nahum. *On the Psalms: Exploring the Prayers of Ancient Israel*. New York: Schocken Books, 1993.

Schaefer, Konrad, OSB. *Psalms*. Berit Olam. Collegeville, MN: Liturgical Press, 2001.

Wesselschmidt, Quentin F. *Psalms 51 – 150*. Ancient Christian Commentary on Scripture. Downers Grove, IL: InterVarsity Press, 2007.